Chawton House Library

'Men have ha
own story. Ea *r*
a degree; the pe
Anne Elliot in Jane A

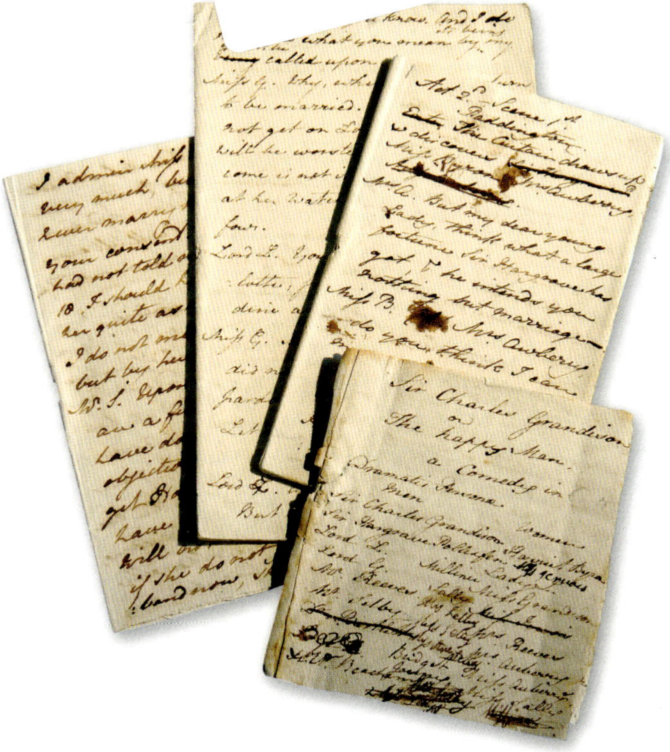

From Medieval Manor to Modern Library

The house that you see today is over four hundred years old, built by the Knight family in the 1580s following the acquisition of the estate by Nicholas Knight in 1578. There was already a manor house on the estate prior to this, first recorded in 1224. The precise footprint of this earlier medieval building is unknown, but some earthworks, and the remnants of what may have been a moat, have been discovered and dated to this period. The current building features walls made of flint, topped by an eighteenth-century brick parapet and a gabled tiled roof. The entrance front, with a three-storey porch, faces west, with the gardens to the south. The other sides of the house present a far from uniform aspect, testifying to centuries of change and development undergone by the building as it passed through different hands.

The manor of Chawton belonged to the English thane Odo until the Norman Conquest, when it was appropriated by William the Conqueror and given to the de Port family, who held it for four generations until Adam de Port married an heiress of the St John family. Sometimes descending through the female line (with concomitant name changes to Poynings, Bonville, Fulford and finally West), the manor remained the property of the St John family and their descendents for nearly four hundred years.

In medieval times, the manor of Chawton was an important stopping place for monarchs travelling between Guildford and London or Winchester. Between 1229 and 1272, for instance, Henry III is known to have visited Chawton twenty-two times. His son Edward I continued the practice of paying visits to Chawton. However, relations between the St John family and the reigning monarch seem to have become more distant, as the last-known royal visit to Chawton was made by Edward III, in 1331.

The Knight family was already leasing the 'cite of the manor place' in Chawton by 1524. The rights were briefly sold to Thomas Arundel in 1558, but it seems likely that the family continued to reside there. At this time, the Knights, farmers of long standing in the Chawton area by the 1570s, were described as 'yeomen' (respectable men of substance just below the rank of gentleman). Nicholas Knight must have been a yeoman of considerable means when in 1578 he paid £720 to acquire from William Arundel the house and the lordship of the manor of Chawton and the right to put forward his chosen

TITLE PAGE
Sir Charles Grandison, a unique manuscript in Jane Austen's own hand.

OPPOSITE
Chawton House, 1834.

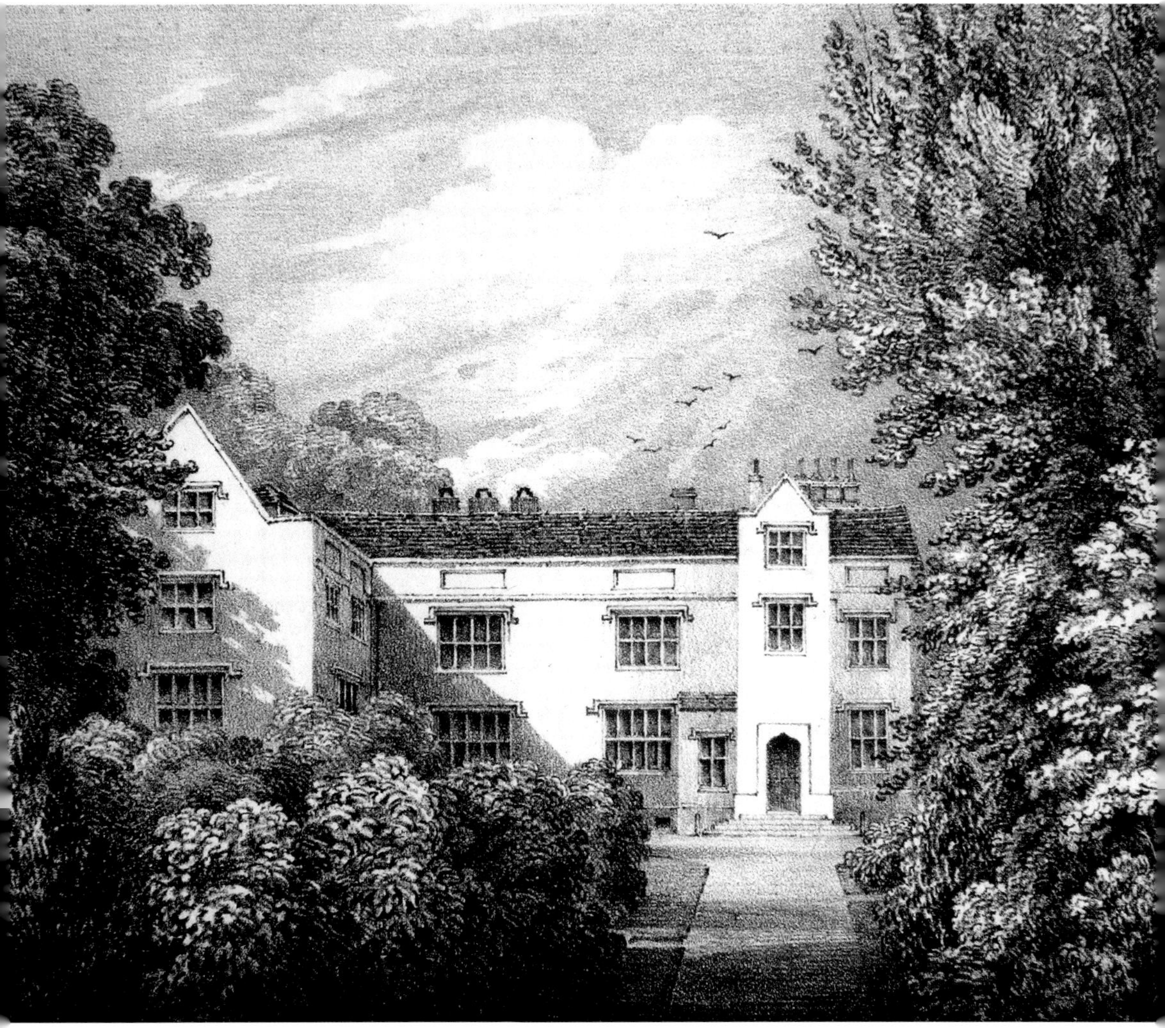

candidate for clerical office here. At that time the manor of Chawton was described as including, as well as the principal buildings and holdings of land, twelve 'tofts' (plots on which peasants' cottages stood), a mill, a dovecot, a quantity of gardens, meadows, pasture, wood and heath. Nicholas had a large family, and his eldest son John now embarked on extensive building operations at the manor house and its stables.

This was a period of rapid change throughout the country. Queen Elizabeth I was on the throne, Sir Francis Drake had circumnavigated the globe, and the nation had recently converted to the new Protestant form of worship. The Knight family in its ascendency played its own part in national affairs from this quiet Hampshire seat. In 1588, John Knight contributed to the funds raised by the Queen in connection with the Spanish Invasion, and in 1609 he became High Sheriff of Hampshire. For those in less

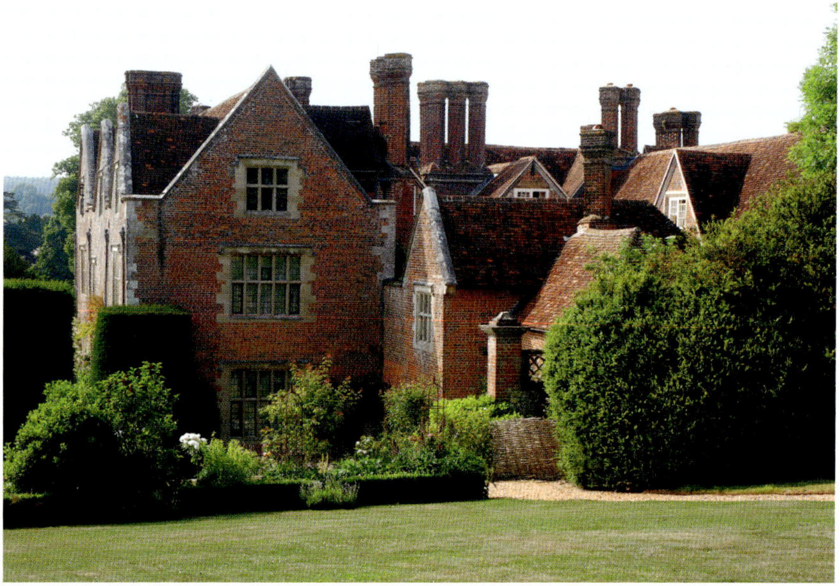

RIGHT The house viewed from the Upper Terrace.

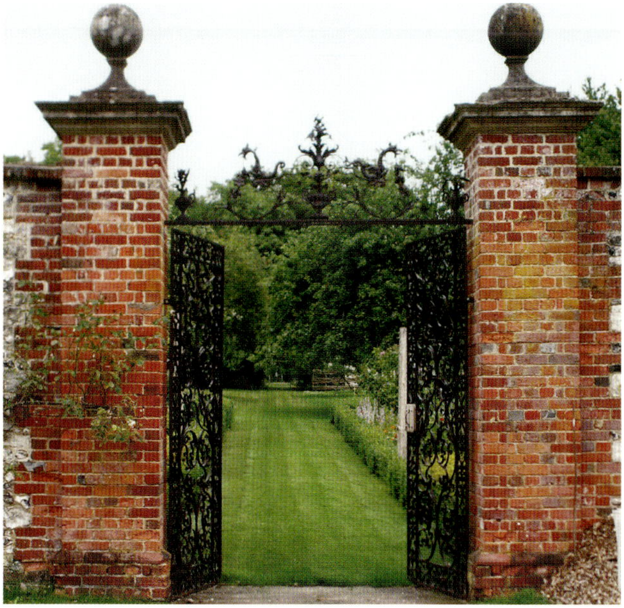

ABOVE The Walled Garden.

RIGHT The Jacobean hanging staircase.

illustrious households, and for most women, the pace of change was felt less keenly. At this time in London only one woman in approximately ten could sign her name, and witchcraft was a capital offence.

The freehold of Chawton House continued to be linked to the Knight name throughout the seventeenth and eighteenth centuries. In order to keep the Chawton freehold in the extended family, title passed laterally and by female descent on several occasions, requiring successive heirs to change their surnames to Knight. This last occurred in 1812–13, some years after control of the estate passed to Edward Austen, who duly changed his surname to Knight. In 1809, Edward's sister Jane Austen (1775–1817) moved into what had been the bailiff's residence, five minutes' walk from Chawton House, and began the most prolific period of her writing life.

In 1826, Chawton House became the home of Edward's son, also Edward, who lived here until he died in 1879. He made many improvements, as did his son Montagu who held the estate until his death in 1914. When Lionel Knight (who inherited next) returned after World

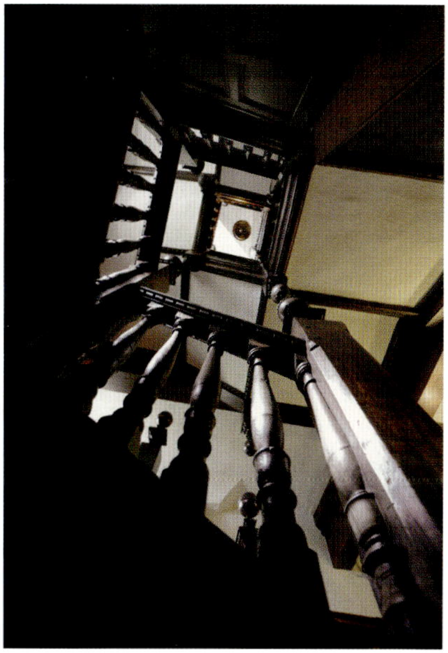

RIGHT Girls and staff from a Barnardo's home in residence during World War II.

BELOW Extensive restoration work was carried out from 1996 until 2003.

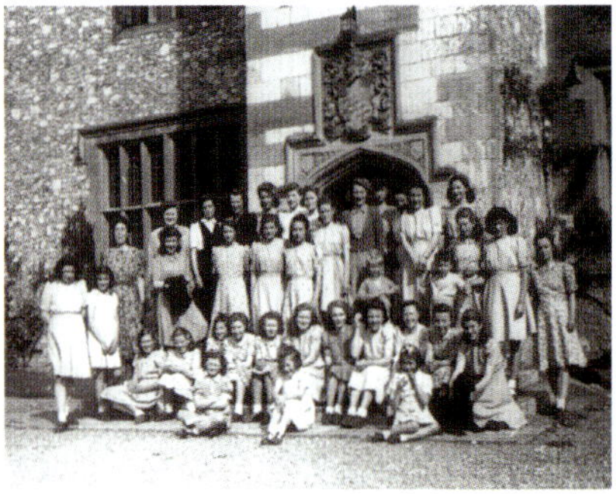

War I, he noted the need for bathrooms, heating and electric light. The house was leased to writer Euphrasia Emeline Cox in 1939, and between 1943 and 1947 part of it was occupied by girls and staff from a Barnardo's Home, which relocated from London during World War II.

Inheritance taxes and high running costs gradually compelled the sale of most of the outlying manor and the subdivision of the house into flats, and, when Richard Knight inherited the house in 1987, he was forced to sell a 125-year lease. The house and estate were initially bought by a property development company with the intention of converting it into a luxury hotel and golf course; the company eventually went into liquidation, however, and the house fell into extreme disrepair. Thankfully, the house's decline was halted in 1993 with the sale of a long lease to a new charity established by the American entrepreneur and philanthropist Sandy Lerner.

The house you see today emerged from a major programme of restoration that spanned the years 1996 to 2003, when it opened as Chawton House Library. When acquired in 1993, the house had stood empty for some years and parts of it were derelict. The initial phase of building work aimed simply at halting the building's decline, while its history was researched and more detailed plans for its restoration were drawn up in negotiation with local planning departments and English

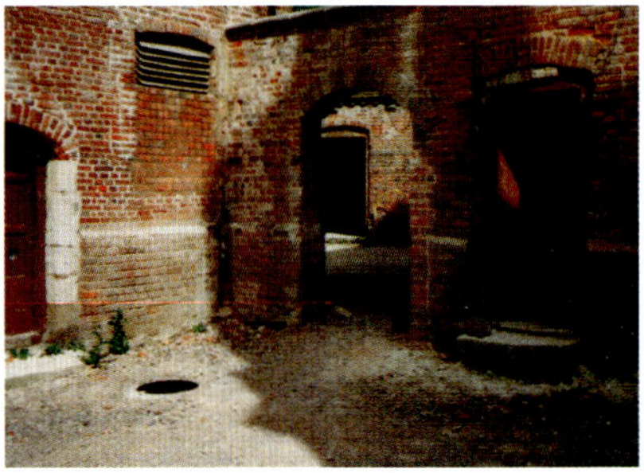

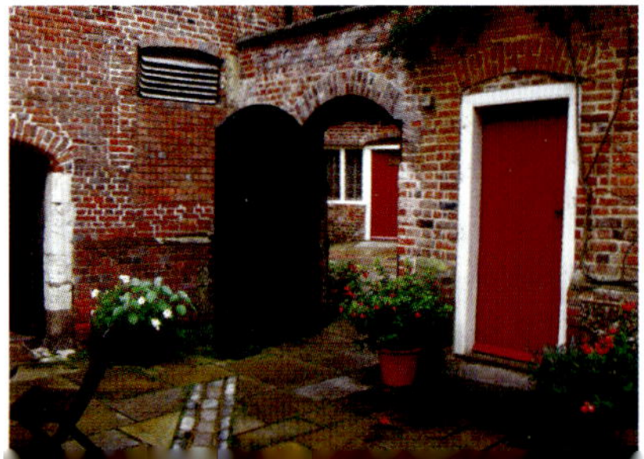

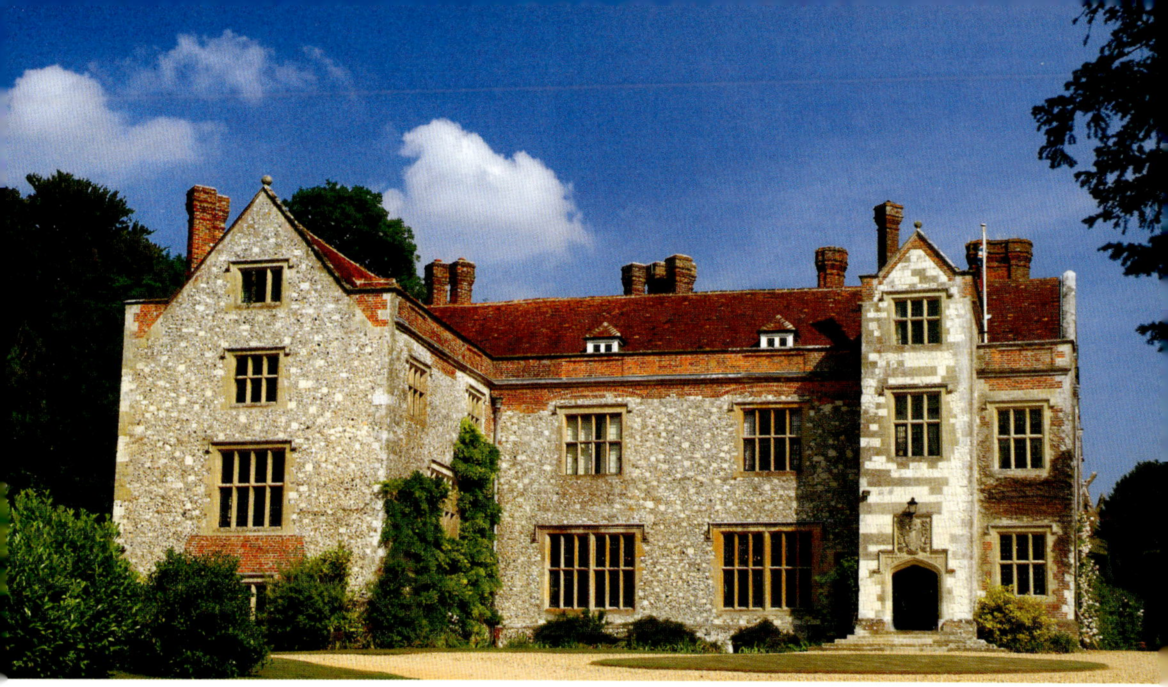

ABOVE Chawton House Library today.

Heritage. Once the necessary consents were obtained, work could begin in earnest. This ranged from renovating the massive timbers of the roof to taking down a Victorian wing that was damaging the fabric of the Elizabethan building. There were plenty of surprises along the way: a long-hidden cupboard, for instance, was found to contain an early-seventeenth-century telescope. The restoration process extended to the grounds, where the aim was to return the gardens and estate to their eighteenth-century appearance. This involved returning the land from arable use to parkland, planting several thousand trees and restoring features such as the 'ha-ha', a landscape-design element that creates a barrier for grazing livestock while preserving an uninterrupted view.

Like many houses of great age, the interior of Chawton House has undergone alteration over the centuries, and the rooms we see today are not always (or even usually) exactly as they appeared in earlier times. The uses to which interior space is put are often fluid, today as in the past. You may be surprised to see no bedrooms, for instance: where a substantial four-poster or a servant's humble truckle-bed once stood, you are likely today to see a dining table or a writing desk. What follows describes simply a particular instant in the life of a house that is sure to carry on evolving over centuries to come.

The Entrance Hall

'I prefer liberty to chains of diamonds.'

Lady Mary Wortley Montagu (1689–1762), letter to Lady Frances Steuart, 1758

RIGHT *Lady Mary Wortley Montagu* by Charles Jervas.

OPPOSITE ABOVE Engraving by George Glover of Penthesilea from Richard Heywood, *The Exemplary Lives and Memorable Acts of Nine the most Worthy Women of the World*, 1640.

OPPOSITE BELOW Frontispiece engraving by George Glover after Sir Anthony van Dyck of Henrietta Maria (1609–1669), Queen of Charles I.

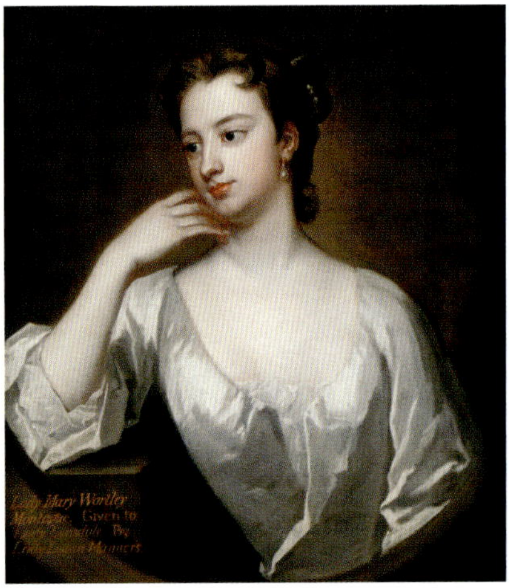

The Entrance Hall was originally part of the Great Hall, which in most houses would have been entered via a screened passage that helped to reduce drafts. At Chawton a screen was put in place for this purpose during the Elizabethan period and later enclosed to form a more permanent division between passage and Great Hall. The leather buckets are from 1726 and came from the family of Bulstrode Peachey, who married into the Knight family in the eighteenth century. They would be taken down in the event of a fire, to be filled from the nearby well.

Presiding over the Entrance Hall is a portrait of Lady Mary Wortley Montagu, poet, essayist, romance-writer and letter-writer, whose work included fascinating letters about life at court in various European countries and in Turkey, where she lived from 1716 to 1718 while her husband was British Ambassador to the Ottoman Empire. On her return to London she campaigned for the introduction of inoculation against smallpox. Her reputation was compromised by this public activism and by her clash in print with the poet Alexander Pope. The Library holds a number of Montagu's works, including a first edition of *The Poetical Works of the Right Honourable Lady M--y W-----y M------e*, published in 1768 after her death.

The focus of Chawton House Library's collection is upon women's writing first and foremost, but some texts particularly relevant to women's experience and perceived place in society are included regardless of the author's sex. One of the earliest of these is also one of the most visually enchanting: Thomas Heywood's *The Exemplary Lives and Memorable Acts of Nine the most Worthy Women of*

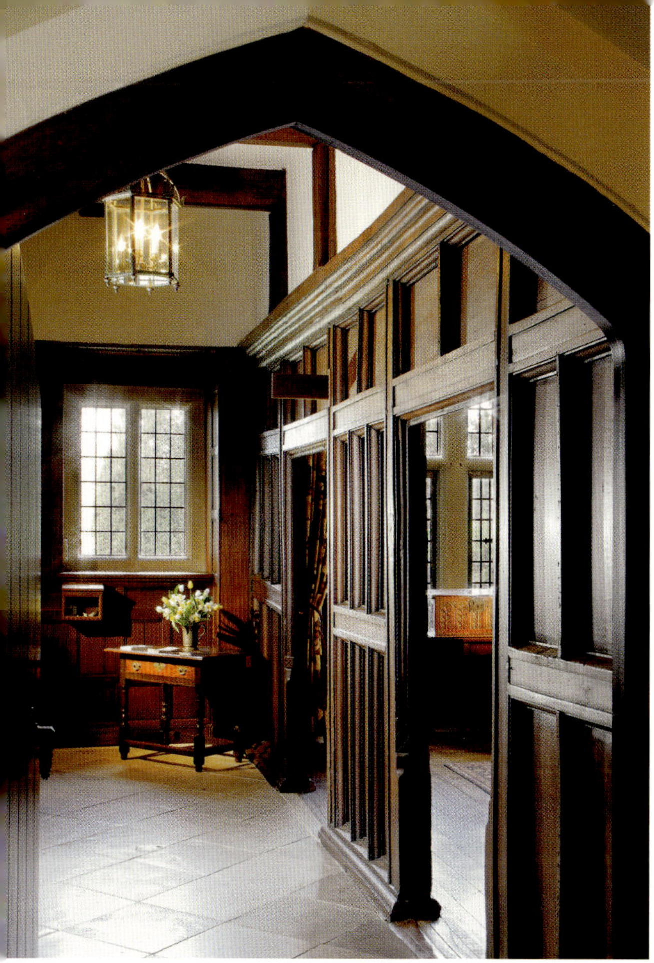

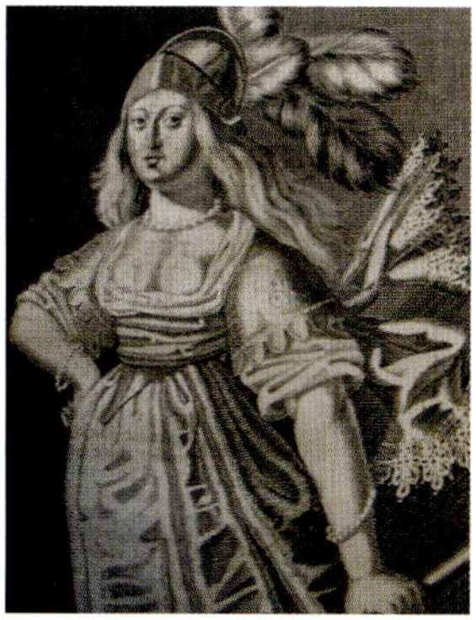

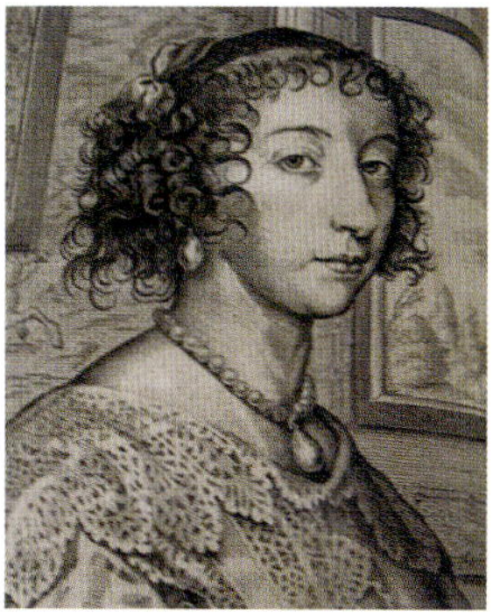

ABOVE Entrance Hall.

the World (1640), regarded by some as a proto-feminist work. This text reminds us that the early modern period was marked by a sometimes uneasy fascination with powerful and indeed warlike women.

Each of the nine women considered by Heywood (1573–1641) is depicted in a vivid engraving by George Glover. Illustrated here is Penthesilea (variously spelled).

This Queen of the Amazons was killed in the Trojan wars by Achilles, who then fell in love with her upon removing her helmet. Heywood describes Penthesilea as 'The first brave Championesse observed in field,/Arm'd with a Polleax and a Mooved Shield'. An altogether more conventional representation of femininity is provided by the book's frontispiece portrait of Henrietta Maria, consort to the ill-fated Charles I. This is a fortunate survival: of the extant copies of this book, few retain this frontispiece engraving.

The Great Hall

'Let me ask the rational and thinking mortal, why the graces of feminine beauty are to be constituted emblems of a debilitated mind?'

Mary Robinson (1758–1800), *A Letter to the Women of England on the Injustice of Mental Subordination*, 1799

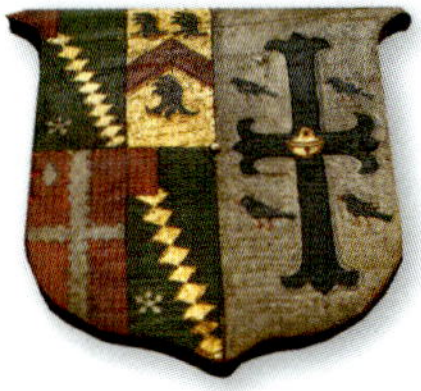

The Great Hall dates from the phase of improvement started by John Knight in 1583; tree-ring analysis reveals that some of the panelling dates from this period and some from the 1620s. A great hall in a building of this age is the descendant of Anglo-Saxon domestic architecture when it had been a space in which servants, master and mistress ate and bedded down for the night. By the 1500s, gentry families lived in something closer to today's idea of privacy, and the great hall was instead an impressive room that proclaimed its owner's status. It is now the Library's principal reception room.

The fireplace, discovered during conservation work, is a remnant of the medieval manor house. Its metal fireback bears the initials 'IK [John Knight] 1588', the year in which England successfully defended itself against the Spanish Armada. It is likely that this commemorative fireback symbolised the support John Knight gave to this campaign. The overmantel depicts four naked figures, two women and two bearded men. Beside the fireplace are some incised apotropaic or ritual marks intended to ward off witches, who were thought to gain entry through window openings, doorways and chimneys. In the adjacent arches and along the panelling are the coats of arms of later Knights. The wooden floor was laid in 1868 in place of an earlier stone floor. Montagu Knight, then aged twenty-four, left under it a message in a bottle that was uncovered in 2001 and is now on display here.

The portraits in the Great Hall, and on the ground floor generally, focus upon women of the long eighteenth century (about 1660 to 1830). In this room they include a portrait believed to be of

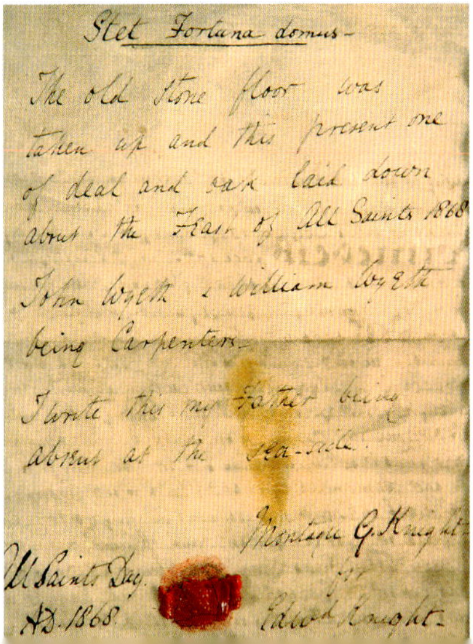

Stet Fortuna domus –

The old stone floor was taken up and this present one of deal and oak laid down about the Feast of All Saints 1868

John Wyeth & William Wyeth being Carpenters –

I write this my Father being absent at the sea-side.

Montagu G. Knight for Edward Knight

All Saints Day AD 1868

ABOVE The coats of arms on the fireplace were probably installed by Montagu Knight.

RIGHT The message in a bottle found under the floor of the Great Hall in 2001.

OPPOSITE *Charlotte Gunning* by George Romney.

Become a Friend of Chawton House Library

When you become a friend of Chawton House Library, you will be helping us to develop our unique collection of books and manuscripts, to continue our Visiting Fellowships and our award-winning schools programme, and to ensure that the work of these women writers lives on. Through your friendship, you will secure the future of this special place for generations to come. You will also receive exclusive benefits:

SARAH FIELDING'S REAL FRIEND

£36 A YEAR OR £3 A MONTH

'A Person who could be trusted, one who was capable of being a real Friend'

Sarah Fielding, *The Adventures of David Simple, in search of a Real Friend* (1744)

AS A TOKEN OF OUR THANKS YOU WILL RECEIVE:

- Welcome Pack, including bookmark
- *The Female Spectator*, our regular newsletter
- One Library tour for you and a guest
- Selected offers for our annual events programme
- An exclusive silver-plated quill pin

FRANCES BURNEY'S HONOURED FRIEND

£120 A YEAR OR £10 A MONTH

'My dear and Honoured Friend... I come to you now without hesitation'

Frances Burney, *Camilla, or a Picture of Youth* (1796)

AS A TOKEN OF OUR THANKS YOU WILL RECEIVE ALL OF THE ABOVE, PLUS:

- An invitation to a special annual event at Chawton House Library

ANN RADCLIFFE'S PRESERVER

£480 A YEAR OR £40 A MONTH

'Ellena could find no words to express her joy and surprise on beholding her preserver'

Ann Radcliffe, *The Italian* (1797)

AS A TOKEN OF OUR THANKS YOU WILL RECEIVE ALL OF THE ABOVE, PLUS:

- Welcome notice in *The Female Spectator*
- An exclusive sterling silver quill pin
- Personal annual update on the collection by the Librarian

THE BLUESTOCKING CIRCLE

LIFETIME MEMBERSHIP
£3,000 MINIMUM DONATION

'The Men not bound by pedant rules Nor Ladies Precieuses ridicules'

Hannah More, *Les Bas-Bleu; or Conversation* (1787)

AS A TOKEN OF OUR THANKS YOU WILL RECEIVE ALL OF THE ABOVE, PLUS:

- Members name recorded in our Book of Bluestockings in the Library
- Recognition and thanks in the Annual Report & Accounts
- An exclusive gold quill pin
- Invitations to Bluestocking Circle events

You can become a Friend at www.chawtonhouselibrary.org, by calling 01420 541010 or by completing the form overleaf and posting it back to us.

We are a registered non-profit in the USA.
Please visit our website to become a North American Friend.

PLEASE SELECT YOUR ANNUAL MEMBERSHIP DONATION:

☐ *Sarah Fielding's* Real Friend (£36 or £3 a month)

☐ *Sarah Fielding's* Real Friend joint membership (£48 or £4 a month)

☐ *Frances Burney's* Honoured Friend (£120 or £10 a month)

☐ *Ann Radcliffe's* Preserver (£480 or £40 a month)

☐ *The Bluestocking Circle* Lifetime Membership £3,000 mininum donation

TITLE FORENAME

SURNAME

ADDRESS

POSTCODE

TELEPHONE

EMAIL

☐ Please keep me informed about your work via email

☐ This is Joint membership

☐ This is Gift membership

PLEASE PROVIDE DETAILS OF JOINT MEMBER/ GIFT RECIPIENT HERE:

TITLE FORENAME

SURNAME

ADDRESS

POSTCODE

EMAIL

☐ I enclose a cheque made payable to *Chawton House Library*

☐ Please charge £ to credit/debit card: Visa/Mastercard/Switch (circle as appropriate)

Card number:

____/____/____/____

Expiry date: __/__

Issue number (switch/maestro only) ____

☐ *Yes, I want to Gift Aid my donation to Chawton House Library*

Gift Aid allows Chawton House Library to reclaim from the tax you pay for the current tax year, to boost your donation by 25p for every £1 you donate.

SIGNATURE

DATE

Signing this declaration indicates that you are a UK taxpayer and that you understand that if you pay less income tax and/or capital gains tax in the current tax year than the amount of Gift Aid claimed on all your donations, it is your responsibility to pay the difference. Please notify Chawton House Library if you want to cancel this declaration, change your name or home address, or you no longer pay sufficient tax on your income and/or capital gains.

Chawton House Library

Please return your completed form and payment to: Chawton House Library, Chawton, Alton, GU34 1SJ

info@chawtonhouselibrary.org 01420 541010
www.chawtonhouselibrary.org
Registered Charity Number 1026921
Registered Company Number 2851718

North American Friends of Chawton House Library (NAFCHL)
Section 501(c)(3) Public Non-Profit

Georgiana, Duchess of Devonshire who wrote poetry, fiction and travel accounts, one of the actor Elizabeth Hartley and another of Queen Charlotte's maid of honour Charlotte Gunning, reportedly given the nickname 'Lady Charlotte Hebrew' for her learning.

Also among the paintings here is John Hoppner's portrait, featured on the back of this guidebook, of the celebrated actor and writer Mary Robinson (1758-1800). Robinson's first work, *Poems* (1775), was published while she was accompanying her husband in a debtors' prison and caring for her baby. The painting was completed around 1782, soon after Robinson became mistress to the Prince of Wales after catching his eye while playing Perdita in *The Winter's Tale*. Her affair with the Prince and her stage career made her a scandalous figure and a celebrity. In 1783 she was paralysed from the waist down, possibly as a result of complications following a miscarriage. Unable to act, she concentrated on writing poetry, novels and plays. The first edition of her novel *Vancenza* (1792) sold out in one day. The Library's collection includes first editions of several of her works and of her *Memoirs* (1801), completed by her daughter and published after her death.

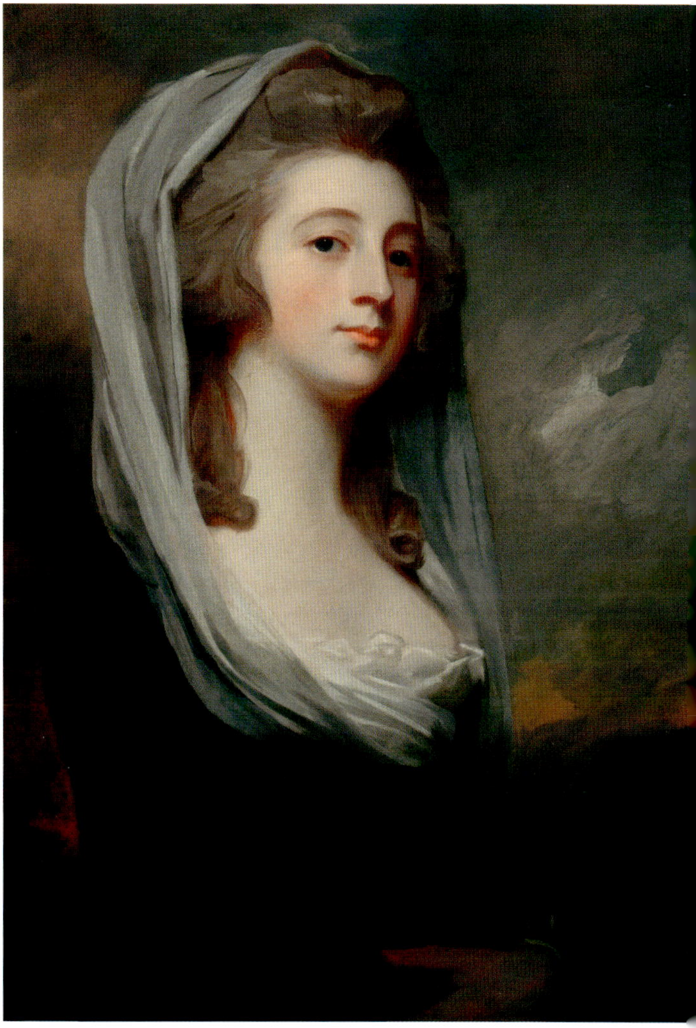

Professional Women Writers

'She resolved to adopt some new mode of obtaining a subsistence; and... determined on making the modern experiment, both for the attainment of fame and profit, by writing a Novel.'

Mary Robinson (1758–1800), *The Natural Daughter* (1799)

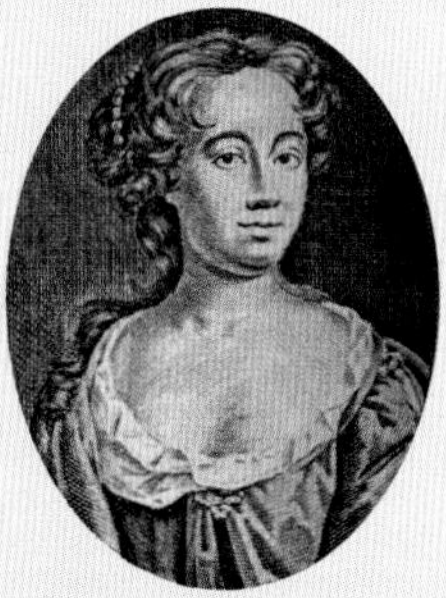

ABOVE Engraving of Aphra Behn after Riley, from *Familiar Letters of Love, Gallantry and Several Other Occasions, by the Wits of the Last and Present Age*, 1724.

Women have always written privately as well as in print, of course, and they have written letters and diaries as well as poetry and fiction. Chawton House Library has a number of manuscripts in its collection, from letters to complete unpublished novels.

Nevertheless, during a period of increased literacy that saw an explosion in English print culture, a growing number of professional women writers emerged. Among the earliest was Aphra Behn (1640–1689), whose name was long disparaged for the sensuality of her writing. From the vantage point of 1929, however, Virginia Woolf was able to write: 'All women together ought to let flowers fall upon the tomb of Aphra Behn which is, most scandalously but rather appropriately, in Westminster Abbey, for it was she who earned them the right to speak their minds.'

For Behn, writing plays, poetry and fiction was not a hobby but an economic necessity. Shrewd commercial judgement dictated her choices, including her translation of a number of French best-sellers such as Bonnecorse's *La Montre* (in Behn's version, *The Lover's Watch*). The Library's copy of this work has a frontispiece engraving of a watch given by the heroine of the story to her absent lover. Its face marks out the languishing postures she expects him to adopt hour by hour.

Encouraging Elizabeth Thomas (1675–1731) to perfect her poetry, John Dryden reassured her 'you, who write only for your Diversion, may pass your Hours with Pleasure in it... always avoiding (as I know you will) the Licenses which Mrs. Behn allowed herself'. The implication is that an author might be tempted to write scandalously because she needed to write what would sell, and Dryden's advice feeds into a more general concern that writing driven by poverty would itself be impoverished.

Another prolific early professional writer was Eliza Haywood (1693–1756), dramatist, poet and novelist with over sixty works of fiction to her name. Haywood also produced one of the first periodical publications by women for women, *The Female Spectator*, which she published from April 1744 to May 1746. Its title a direct play on its famous predecessor *The Spectator*, Haywood's journal was widely read and featured an array of social and political commentary covering everything from the craze for tea drinking and the problem of gambling to politics, war and diplomacy and the importance of science and natural history. The journal also featured romantic and satirical fiction.

Fiction seemed to offer opportunities for women to enter the literary sphere, for writing (or reading) a novel did not require the classical education widely reserved for men. Over a century after Behn had written 'for bread', the great practitioner of the novel, Jane Austen, owned to her niece Fanny that she took pleasure in earning money from her fiction: 'tho' I like praise as well as anybody, I like what [brother] Edward calls *Pewter* too'. It is sobering, however, that her earnings from a lifetime of writing amounted to no more than the sum her clergyman father would have earned in a year. In contrast, Frances Burney (1752–1840), whose first novel, *Evelina, or, a Young Lady's Entrance into the World*, made her a literary celebrity once the secret of its (anonymous) authorship slipped out, went on to receive the astonishing sum of £1,000 for the copyright of *Camilla: or, a Picture of Youth*, published in 1796. Two dramatic scenes from this novel are depicted in small oil paintings by Henry Singleton (1766–1839) in the Library's collection.

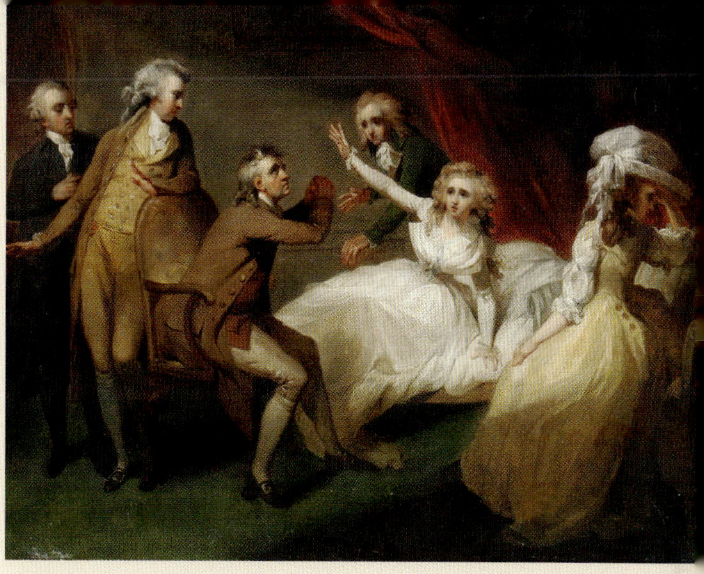

ABOVE *Camilla Recovering from her Swoon* by Henry Singleton.

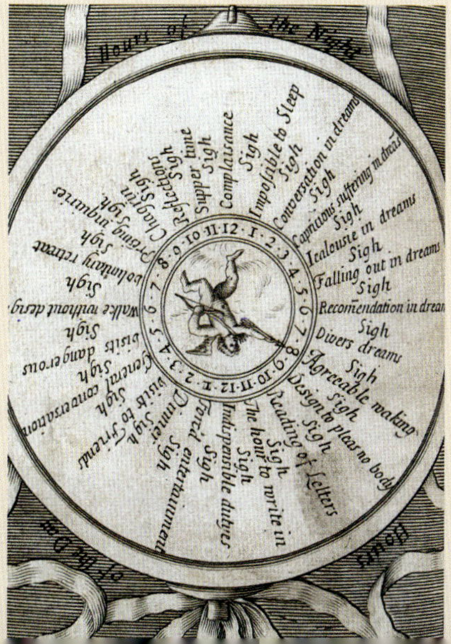

LEFT Engraved frontispiece to Aphra Behn, *The Lover's Watch*, 1686.

The Dining Room

'We four sweet Brothers & Sisters dine today at the Gt House. Is not that quite natural?'

Jane Austen, letter to Caroline Austen, 1815

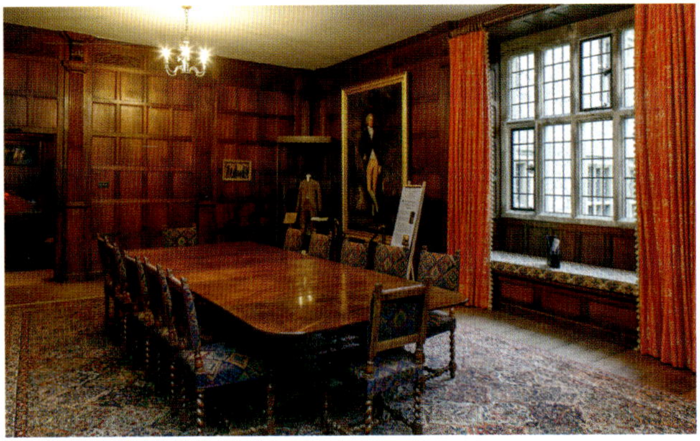

ABOVE The Dining Room.

The Dining Room is the Library's second largest reception room. The paintings just outside this room include a portrait of the courtesan Catherine Fisher (immortalised in the nursery rhyme 'Lucy Locket lost her pocket, Kitty Fisher found it'). Another, titled simply *A Lady*, is said to represent the poet Eleanor Verney, whose tragic death as a teenage bride inspired poems by Lady Mary Wortley Montagu and Mary Astell (1666–1731).

The panelling and ornate fireplace in the Dining Room mark the silver wedding of Montagu and Florence Knight, whose initials appear with the date 1895 on the wooden panel above the fireplace. The Knight family dining table belonged to Edward Austen, later Knight, and has been loaned to the Library by Richard Knight, the current freeholder. It is almost certain that Jane Austen sat at this table when dining at the 'Great House'.

Among the paintings in the Dining Room is a 1783 silhouette by William Wellings (see p.27) depicting the young Edward Austen's first introduction to Thomas and Catherine Knight, who later made him their heir, thereby bringing Chawton House into Jane Austen's immediate family. Another painting features Catherine Sophia Macaulay, daughter of the radical historian and philosopher Catharine Macaulay (1731–1791), with her mother's admirer Thomas

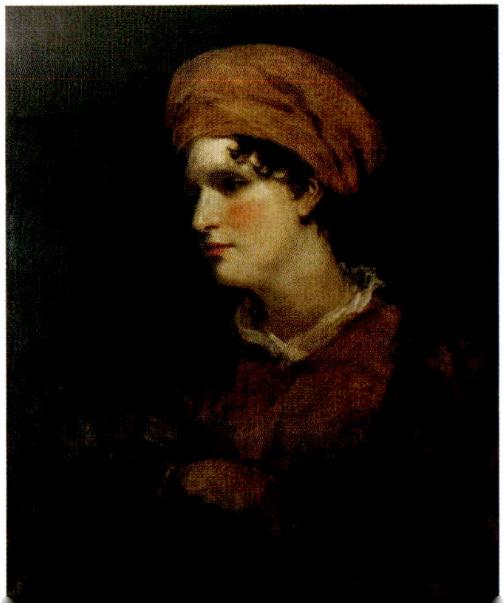

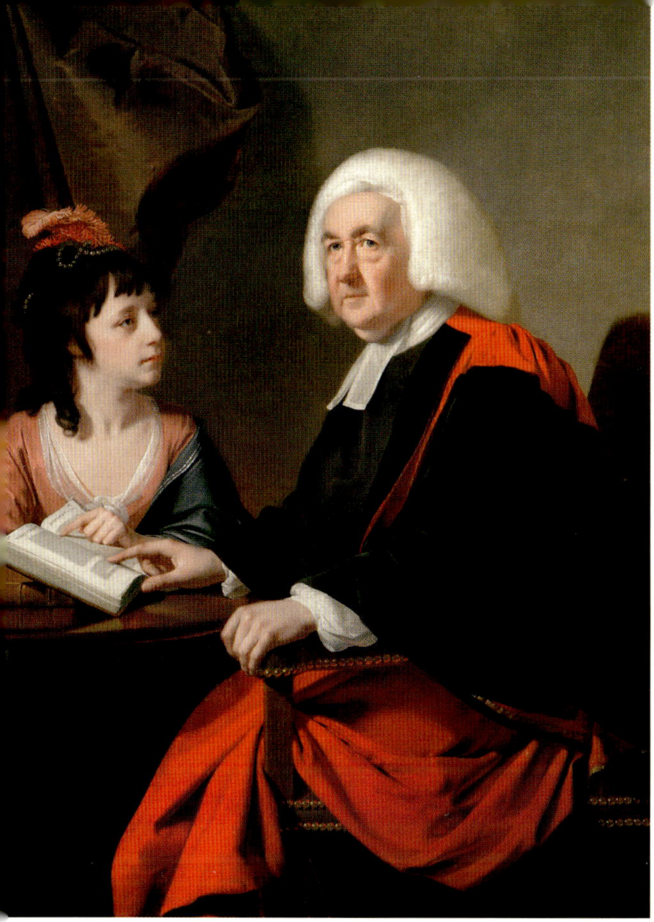

ABOVE *The Reverend Thomas Wilson and Catherine Sophia Macaulay* by Joseph Wright 'of Derby'.

LEFT Portrait of Maria Graham by John Jackson RA.

Wilson. The wealthy Rev. Wilson invited Macaulay and her daughter to live in his house in Bath in 1774, later making Catherine Sophia his heir. Volumes of Macaulay's *History of England from the Accession of James I to the Elevation of the House of Hanover* can be seen in the painting. The first republican history of Britain, it was published from 1763 to 1783 in eight volumes. The Library holds an early edition of each. Macaulay visited the recently established United States of America in 1784–5, where she stayed for ten days with George Washington at Mount Vernon, and her *History* influenced Mercy Otis Warren's *History of the American Revolution*. In a letter discovered only twenty years ago, Mary Wollstonecraft wrote: 'I respect Mrs Macaulay Graham because she contends for laurels whilst most of her sex seek only for flowers.'

A portrait of Maria Graham, later Lady Callcott (1785–1842), also hangs in the Dining Room. Graham published a series of vivid and, by the standards of the time, open-minded travel journals, documenting her time in Brazil, Chile, India and Italy. Graham was also a ground-breaking art historian and author of one of the most popular children's books of all time, *Little Arthur's History of England* (1835).

On display in the Dining Room, alongside his portrait, is a silk frock coat and breeches from 1789 thought to have belonged to Edward Austen (later Knight); they have been painstakingly conserved to stabilise their condition. Next to this clothing is Edward's journal documenting a tour through France to Switzerland in 1786.

Writing and Travel

'I shall endeavour faithfully to describe whatever I see, and carefully to report whatever I learn... I mean to paint from the life, and to adhere to the sober colouring of nature.'
Maria Graham, *Journal of a Residence in India*, 1812

There is an additional surviving travel journal of Edward Austen (later Knight) which describes a journey from Genoa to The Hague in 1790. This was presumably the final stage of his Grand Tour, which was a desirable part of the Georgian gentleman's education. The Tour typically took the form of an extended visit to continental Europe that might absorb a few months or a few years – in the case of James Caulfeild, first Earl of Charlemont, nine years.

During the course of the eighteenth century and beyond, the Tour gradually became less of a male preserve; it was increasingly common to see women and families making the journey. Mariana Starke (*c.*1762–1838) pioneered the guidebook genre with *Letters from Italy* in 1800. *First Impressions on a Tour upon the Continent in the Summer of 1818* by Marianne Baillie (*c.*1795–1831) was another of the earliest accounts of a woman's experience of this form of travel.

In the decade from 1789, travel of a quite different kind took politically engaged women authors to Revolutionary France to experience events there first hand. In England there was enthusiasm for the French Revolution in its early stages and an appetite for news of its developments. Helen Maria Williams wrote an eight-volume account of the Revolution, which she witnessed for herself after settling in France. The first volume, *Letters Written in France in the Summer 1790* (1790), is framed as a series of letters to a friend in England and develops the story of one particular

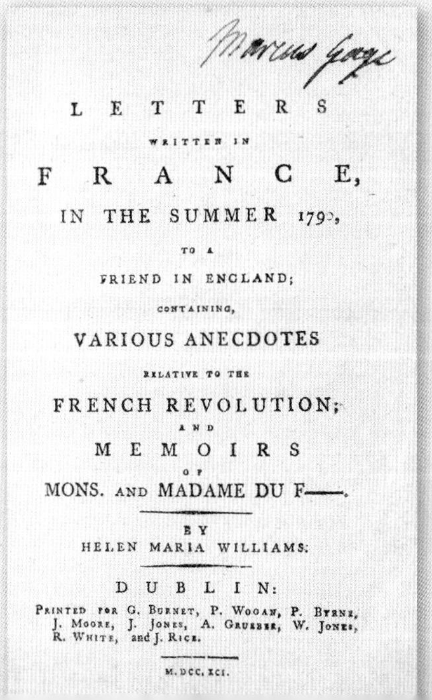
LETTERS
WRITTEN IN
FRANCE,
IN THE SUMMER 1790,
TO A
FRIEND IN ENGLAND;
CONTAINING,
VARIOUS ANECDOTES
RELATIVE TO THE
FRENCH REVOLUTION;
AND
MEMOIRS
OF
MONS. AND MADAME DU F——.
BY
HELEN MARIA WILLIAMS.
DUBLIN:
PRINTED FOR G. BURNET, P. WOGAN, P. BYRNE, J. MOORE, J. JONES, A. GRUEBER, W. JONES, R. WHITE, and J. RICE.
M.DCC.XCI.

RIGHT The title page to Helen Maria Williams' *Letters Written in France*, 1791.

OPPOSITE Lithograph from Marianne Baillie's *First Impressions on a Tour upon the Continent in the Summer of 1818*, 1819.

OPPOSITE FAR RIGHT Detail from Edward Austen's 1786 travel journal.

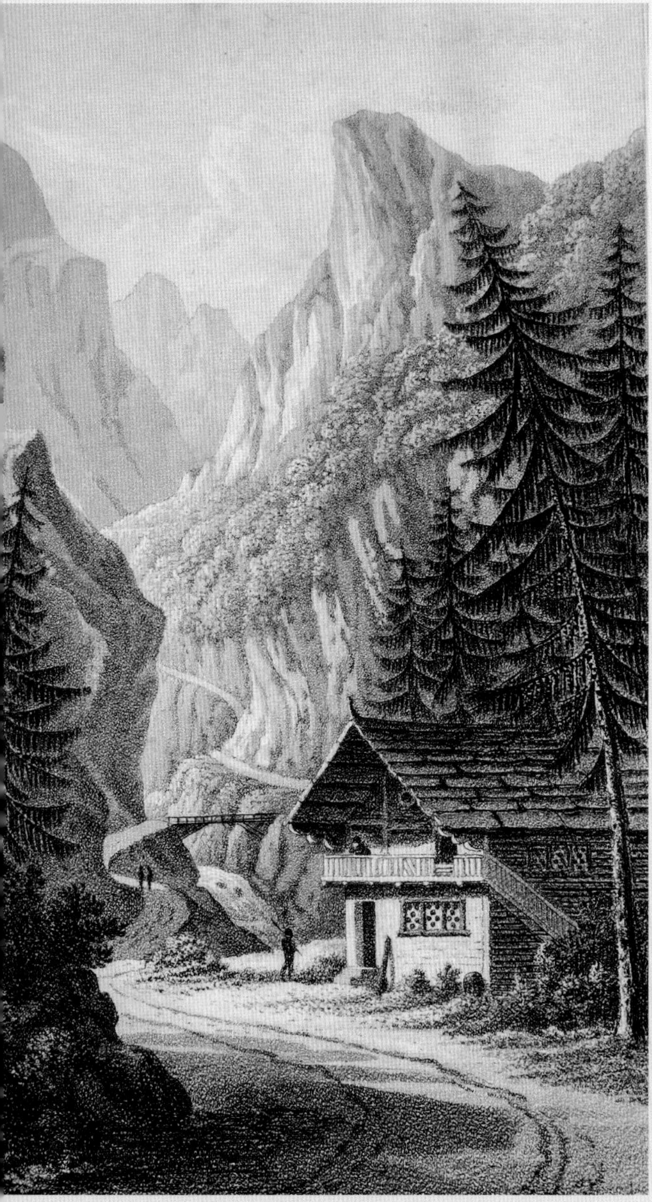

family in order to strengthen the reader's conviction that the Ancien Régime, as it became known, needed to be swept away. It is an account full of hope for the future.

Fictional letters are also the vehicle for the story of an Englishman who is persuaded of the justice of the revolutionary cause by his travels to France in Charlotte Smith's novel *Desmond* (1792). In the two years that had elapsed since Williams's *Letters*, however, attitudes towards events in France had begun to change, and radical sentiment was no

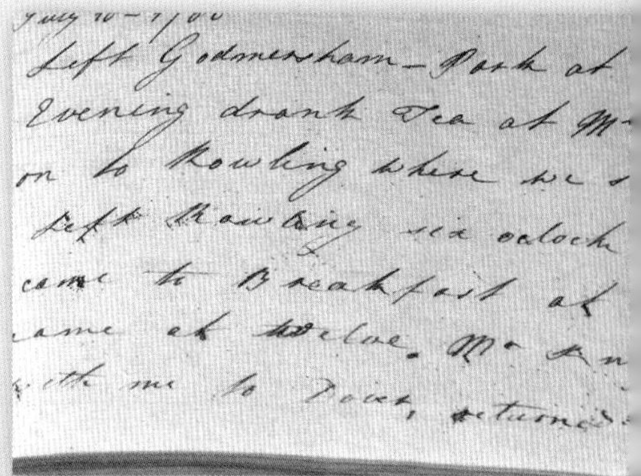
Left Godmersham-Park at
Evening drank Tea at M
on to Rowling where we
Left Rowling six oclock
came to Breakfast at
came at twelve. Mr
with me to Dover, returned

longer guaranteed a sympathetic hearing. With numerous children to support, and despite her considerable standing as a writer, Smith's earnings seem to have been compromised by her continued identification with the revolutionary cause.

The Tapestry Gallery

'Their apartments are adorned with hangings of the finest tapestry of Brussels.'

Lady Mary Wortley Montagu, letter to the Countess of ---- ----, 1716

BELOW LEFT & RIGHT
Portraits of Thomas and Jane Knight by Michael Dahl.

The Tapestry Gallery is situated over what was originally the main staircase for the house as a whole. The tapestries were sold long ago, sadly, to meet household costs. An armorial tapestry dating from 1564 and thought to have been woven in Flanders, or at least by Flemish weavers, was long treasured at Chawton House, where it hung in the Lower Reading Room. It has been in the collection of the Metropolitan Museum of Art in New York since 1958, where it is known as the Lewknor table carpet (after the Lewknor or Lewkenor family, connections of the Knights, for whom it was made).

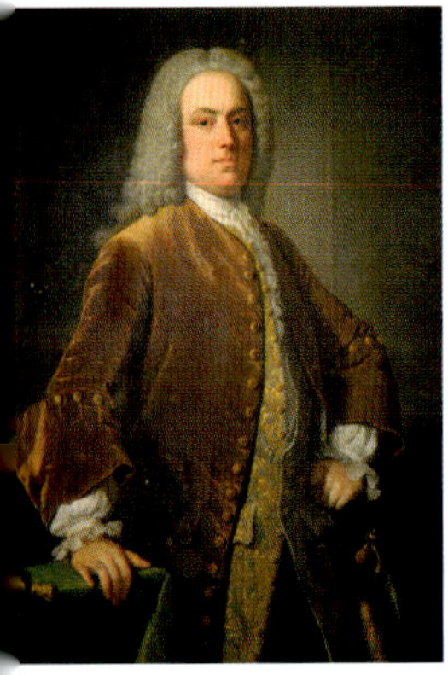

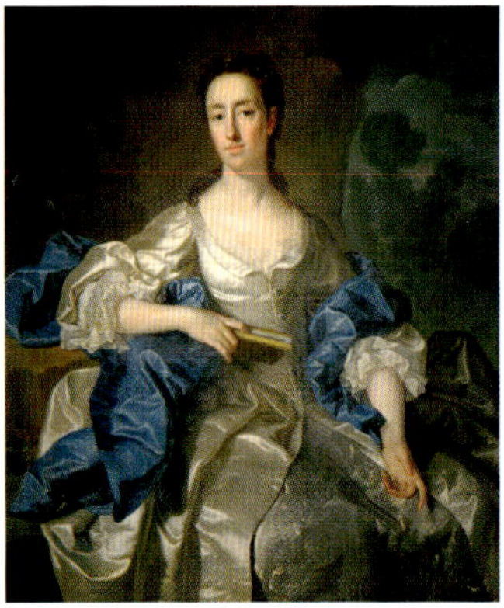

The principal painting in the Tapestry Gallery is of Chawton House in about 1740, signed simply 'Mellichamp'. Nothing is currently known about Mellichamp, who may have been one of the many journeyman artists who would offer their services as they travelled around the country. In a corner of the painting the words 'Mary Jane Austen 1819' appear faintly in pencil: it seems that Mary Jane, eldest child of Jane Austen's brother Francis and twelve years old in 1819, was given to doodling.

Portraits of Thomas Knight and his wife Jane (née Monk) hang in the Gallery. Thomas changed his name twice for the purposes of inheritance, first from Brodnax to May on inheriting Godmersham Park in Kent and then from May to Knight on inheriting the estates of Chawton and Steventon in 1737. It was when Thomas and Jane's only son Thomas Knight II and his wife Catherine realised that they would not have children of their own that they took steps to make the young Edward Austen their heir. Edward was a third cousin on Jane Monk's side of the family. The portraits

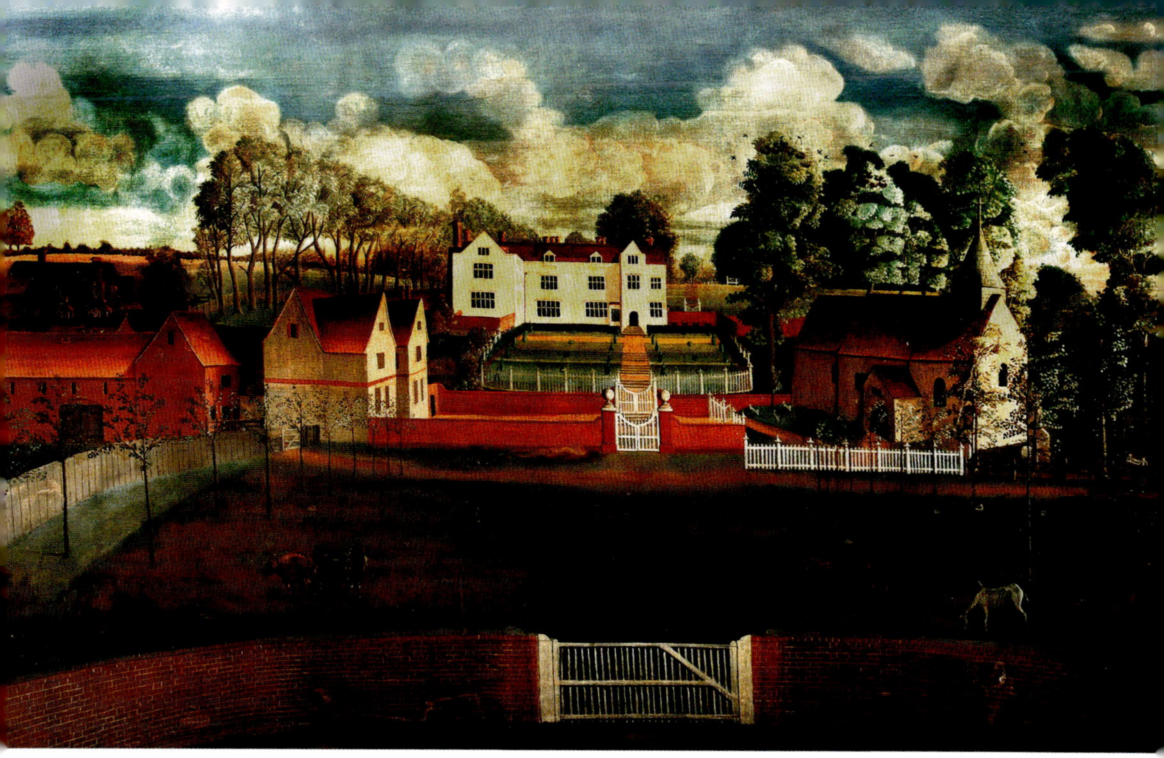

ABOVE Painting of Chawton House by 'Mellichamp', *c.*1740.

RIGHT The original staircase for the house as a whole.

of Thomas Knight II and his mother Jane were recently found to have small cards tucked into the backs of their frames, on which an eighteenth-century hand has detailed the history and parentage of both sitters.

Above the staircase hangs a portrait of an unidentified boy from the Knight family, dating from about 1635. Two portraits in the Gallery itself depict children of the Lewkenor or Lewknor family. The Lewkenors were ancestors of three successive owners of the manor of Chawton in the late seventeenth and early eighteenth centuries.

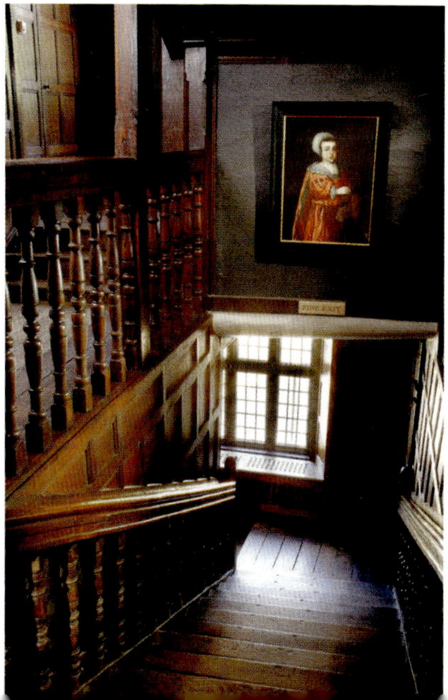

Writing for and about Children

'As nothing can be of more Use to Society than the taking early Care to form the Minds of Youth, I publish some of the verses written by Me with that View... as the best Apology a Woman could make for writing at all.'

Mary Barber (*c.*1685–1755), preface to *Poems on Several Occasions*, 1734

When the Lewkenor children were growing up, young readers relied mainly upon chapbooks for literary entertainment, slight books that recycled old stories from folklore. During the eighteenth century, however, the Enlightenment interest in education ushered in a new strand of literature written expressly for children, often by women. The commercial potential of literature like this was quickly grasped by entrepreneurial publishers like John Newbery (1713–1767).

Irish poet Mary Barber, married to a Dublin draper, was one of a number of women writers who took Jonathan Swift's relatively uncomplicated metre as a model for her poetry. She published *Poems on Several Occasions* in 1734 after raising funds through subscription. A number of the poems were written for her son Constantine to recite, including 'Written for my Son, and spoken by him in School, upon his Master's first bringing in a Rod'. One of the earliest novels specifically for a juvenile readership was *The Governess: or, The Little Female Academy* (1749) by Sarah Fielding, whose brother was the writer Henry Fielding. This 'first children's school story exclusively about and for young girls' remained popular throughout the century. Chawton House Library's copy dates from 1781.

A real rather than fictional governess was among a number of women who wrote thoughtfully about education in general and girls' education in particular. *Private Education, or, a Practical Plan*

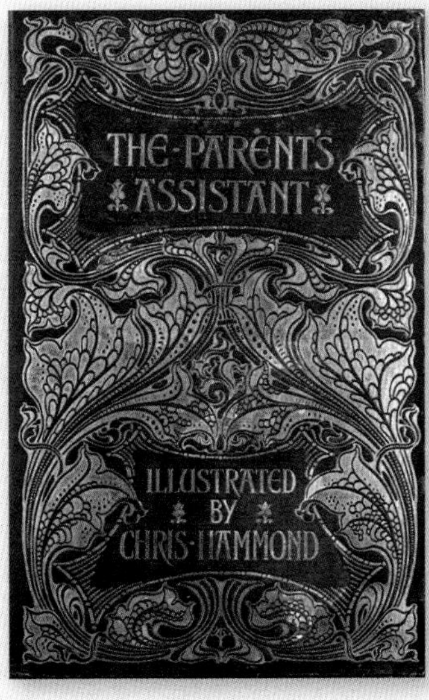

RIGHT Maria Edgeworth's writing for children was hugely popular throughout the nineteenth century. This is an 1897 edition of *The Parent's Assistant*, first published in 1796.

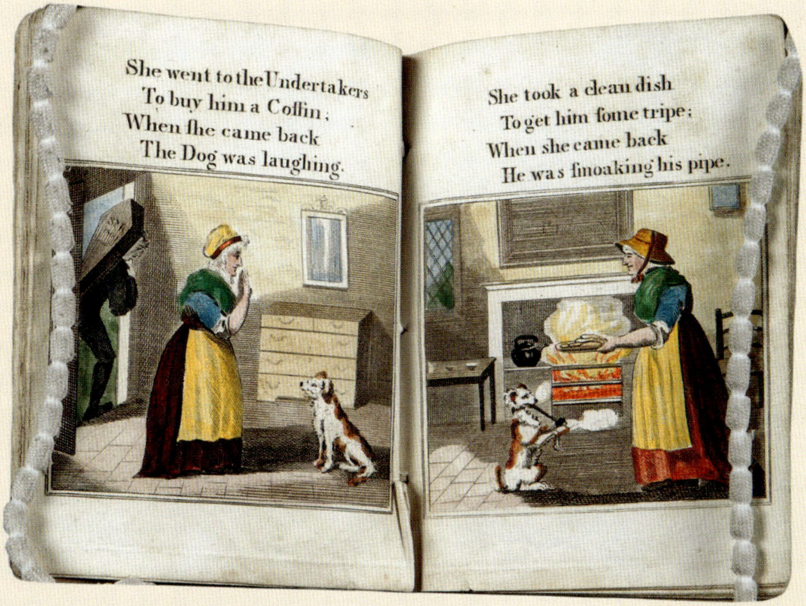

RIGHT Hand-coloured engraving from *The Comic Adventures of Old Mother Hubbard and her Dog* by Sarah Catherine Martin, 1805.

for the Studies of Young Ladies (1815) by Elizabeth Appleton (*c.*1790–1849) advocated a thorough education that did not shy away from demanding subjects like astronomy; her text set out practical, age-appropriate models for parents and educators to follow. The foremost female educationalist of her day, however, was Maria Edgeworth (1768–1849), who co-authored *Essays on Practical Education* (1798) with her father Richard. At the peak of her fame Edgeworth was the most commercially successful and influential writer in England and in Ireland (where members of her family were landowners). Her fiction included *Castle Rackrent* (1800) and *Belinda* (1802). The Library has in its keeping a silver inkstand dating from 1845 that once belonged to Edgeworth. It was brought to Chawton House Library by the late Sir Howard Colvin, whose wife Christina, née Butler, was the editor of Edgeworth's letters and a descendant of the Edgeworth family.

Sarah Catherine Martin's tiny volume *The Comic Adventures of Old Mother Hubbard and her Dog* (1805) has a hand-coloured engraving to accompany each four-line verse. Ironically the colour was usually applied to books like this by apprentices who were themselves children.

The Study and Exhibition Rooms

'Emma has been meaning to read more ever since she was twelve years old. I have seen a great many lists of her drawing up at various times of books that she meant to read regularly through–and very good lists they were–very well chosen and very neatly arranged–sometimes alphabetically and sometimes by some other rule.'

Mr Knightley in Jane Austen's *Emma*, 1816

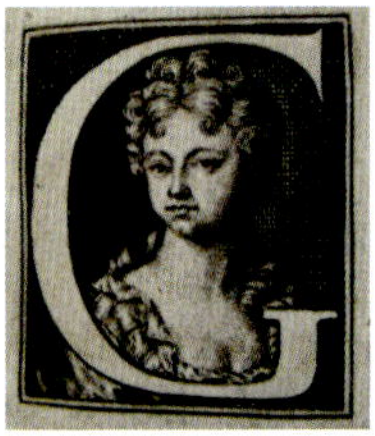

ABOVE Engraved portrait by Simon Gribelin of Elizabeth Elstob.

RIGHT This 1833 American edition of Jane Austen's *Emma* attests to the global appeal of the novel; a theme we explored in our '*Emma* at 200' exhibition.

Until divided in the mid-seventeenth century, the Study Room and the adjacent Exhibition Room would originally have been one space, a 'Great Chamber'. The Elizabethan fireplaces that survive in these rooms gesture to the Great Chamber's importance; it would have been the principal room in the house, where important family occasions took place.

The Study Room serves as an extra space for research and discussion outside the Upper and Lower Reading Rooms. It is used by Visiting Fellows and day researchers and for seminars. A small team of volunteer cataloguers often work here on our collection of modern books, many of which have been donated by supporters of Chawton House Library.

The life and research of an unusual early-eighteenth-century scholar, Elizabeth Elstob (1683–1756), reminds us of some of the obstacles in the path of an eighteenth-century woman who wished to pursue academic study. Brought up by an uncle who was initially opposed to her education, Elizabeth mastered several ancient and modern languages. She is best known for her translation of Aelfric's life of Pope Gregory the Great, *An English-Saxon Homily on the Birthday of St. Gregory* (1709), and for *The Rudiments of Grammar for the English-Saxon Tongue* (1715), both in the Library's collection. Her tiny portrait by Simon Gribelin, no larger than a postage stamp, appeared in both books. In her early life Elstob had the support of her brother, himself

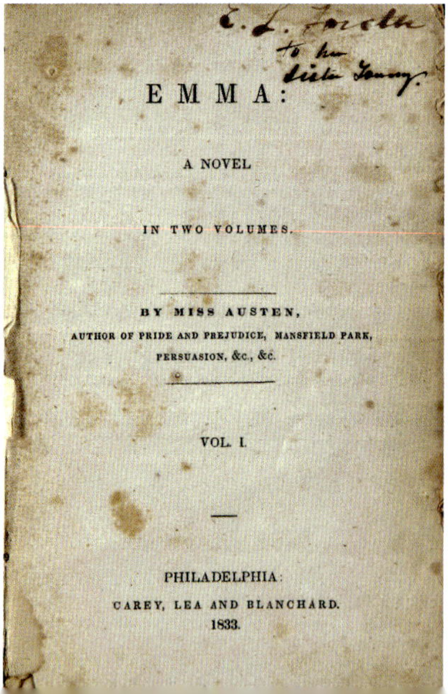

EMMA:

A NOVEL

IN TWO VOLUMES.

BY MISS AUSTEN,

AUTHOR OF PRIDE AND PREJUDICE, MANSFIELD PARK, PERSUASION, &c., &c.

VOL. I.

PHILADELPHIA:

CAREY, LEA AND BLANCHARD.

1833.

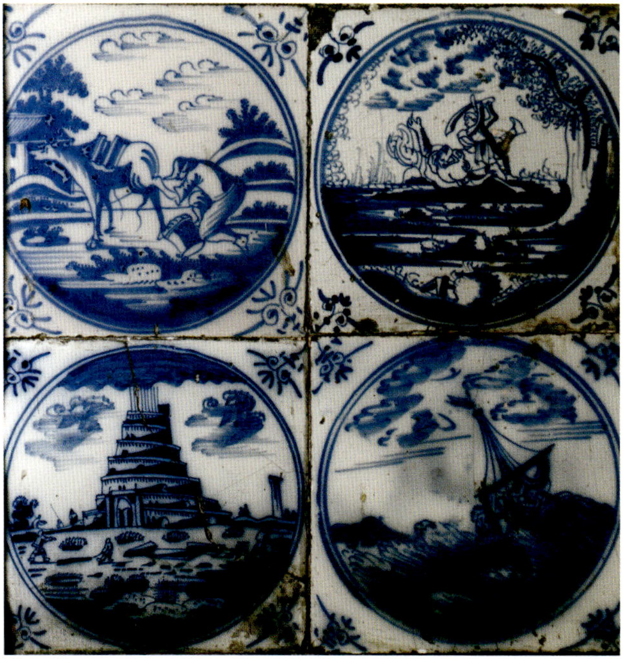

ABOVE Delft tiles surround the fireplace in the Exhibition Room.

a scholarly man, but his untimely death left her in penury. She found security for the last part of her life as a governess in an aristocratic household. Elstob was a major force behind George Ballard's *Memoirs of Several Ladies of Great Britain who have been celebrated for their writings or skill in the learned languages, arts and sciences* (1752). She strengthened Ballard's 'feminist' impulses and handed over the research she had begun herself into historical achievements by women.

The chance survival of a tradesman's bill from the 1820s (for remedying a problem with a chimney) tells us that the Exhibition Room served at that time as the bedroom of Edward Austen (later Knight). The green tiles in the fireplace surround are a late-Victorian or early-Edwardian addition, whilst the blue-and-white tiles are delftware, likely to be a mixture of Dutch and English, dated to the latter half of the eighteenth century. The delftware tiles depict scenes from the Bible.

The Exhibition Room was extensively refurbished in 2016 thanks to funding from the Garfield Weston Foundation, creating a much-needed permanent exhibition space at the Library. Along with new display cases throughout the house, the space in the Exhibition Room allows the Library not only to display many of its own treasures but also to borrow items from other institutions. The first Exhibition held here after the refurbishment was '*Emma* at 200' – a celebration of the bicentenary of the publication of Jane Austen's *Emma*. This exhibition included our own first edition of *Emma*, a number of foreign first editions loaned from overseas institutions and some unique manuscript material. Among the display items was as an original letter by Charlotte Brontë in which she wrote about *Emma*, loaned from the Huntington Library in California.

The Oak Room

'When dinner was over, Mrs. Beaumont recommended the gentlemen to the care of Lord Orville, and then attended the ladies to the drawing-room.'

Frances Burney (1752–1840) *Evelina, or the History of a Young Lady's Entrance into the World*, 1778

The Oak Room gets its name from the fireback, which depicts the oak tree in which King Charles II hid after the Battle of Worcester in 1651. Referred to as 'the Chamber over the Buttery' in accounts from 1619, and as 'the Pantry Chamber' in 1707 bills, it was later used as the 'Ladies' Withdrawing Room'. The room was remodelled around 1900 by Montagu Knight, who installed full-length panelling and a fireplace designed by Sir Edwin Lutyens in malmstone (meaning 'chalky rock').

The Oak Room windows offer excellent views down the drive and over the lawns. From up here the late-eighteenth-century remodelling of earlier, more formal gardens along English Landscape principles is clear to see. This taste for creating what would appear to be a naturalistic landscape extended to crafting the perfect view, either opening a vista by carefully

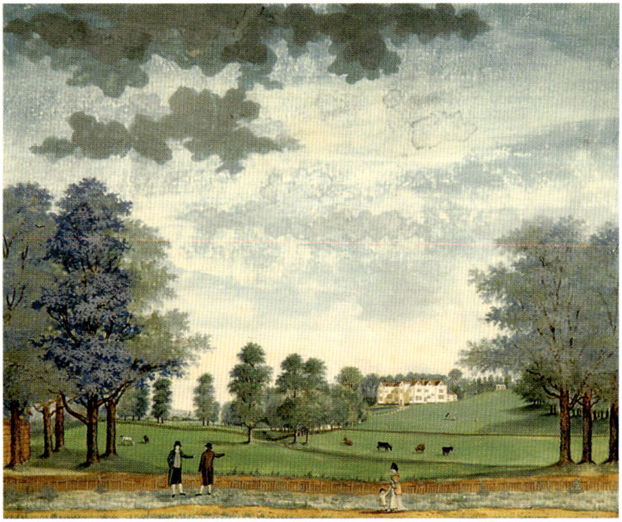

RIGHT *The Great House and Park at Chawton* by Adam Callander, *c.*1780.

OPPOSITE ABOVE Portrait thought to be of Maria Cosway, circle of Richard Cosway.

OPPOSITE RIGHT The Reading Alcove.

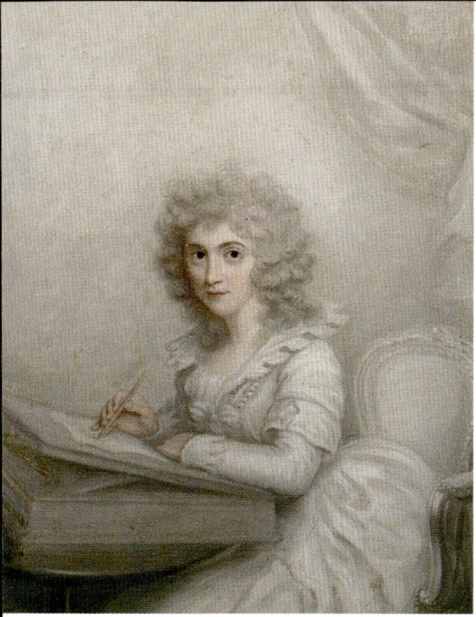

removing trees or, conversely, planting new groups of trees with precision. The new style is captured in the *c.*1780 gouache by Adam Callander, which shows the farmland, lawns and house from the old Gosport Road (now the A32).

On display in the Oak Room is a portrait believed to be of Maria Cosway (1760–1838), an artist and educator. Her history paintings and character portraits were highly regarded, but her status as an artist was curtailed by the refusal of her husband, the artist Richard Cosway, to allow her to sell her work. 'Had Mr. C. permitted me to paint professionally,' she wrote, 'I should have made a better painter.' Increasingly religious in later life, she turned her energies to education, establishing a girls' school in Lyons in 1803 while living in France.

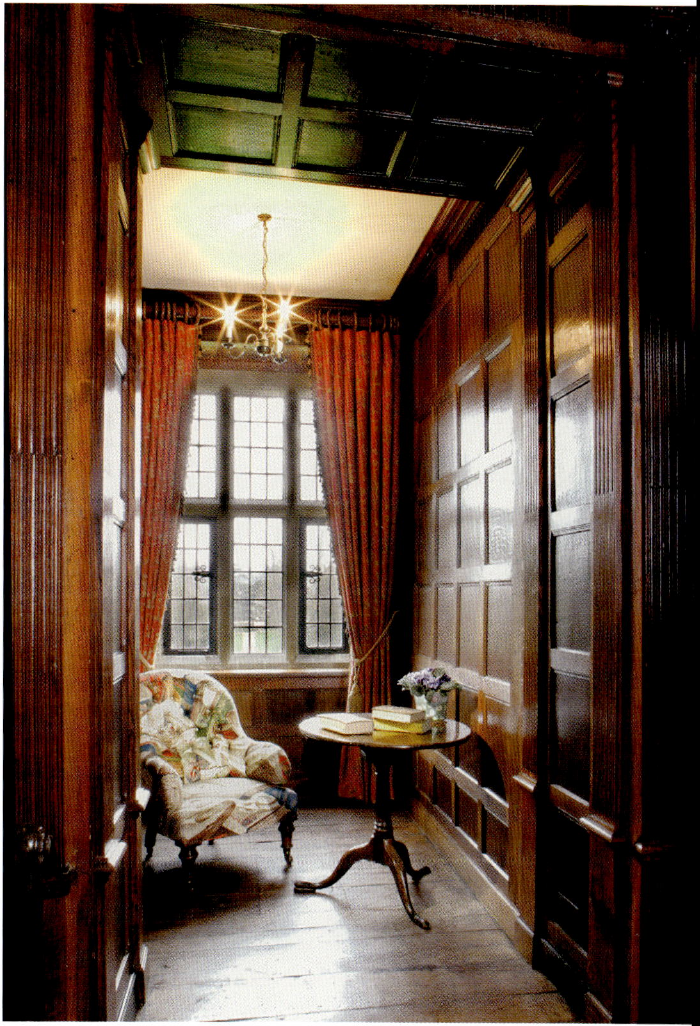

Jane Austen and Chawton House

'I went up to the Great House between 3 & 4, & dawdled away an hour very comfortably.'

Jane Austen, letter to Cassandra Austen, 1814

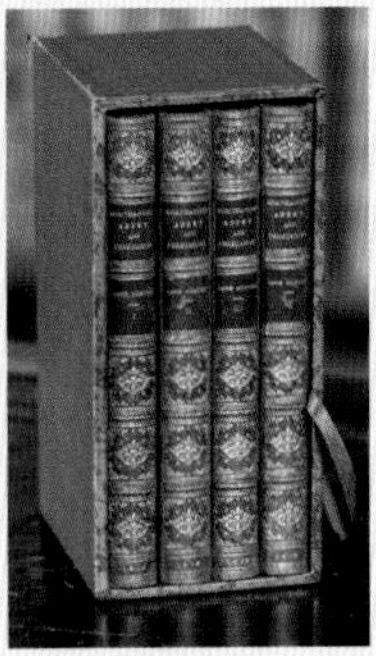

ABOVE Chawton House Library's first edition of Jane Austen's *Northanger Abbey* and *Persuasion* (1817).

According to Knight family legend, Jane Austen used to enjoy sitting in the Oak Room alcove looking down the drive when she visited. We cannot be sure of this, but her letters do indicate that she seems to have regarded Chawton House almost as an extension of her own home, passing on domestic news no matter how trivial ('The chimneys at the Great House are done', she writes to her sister Cassandra).

When her brother Edward became heir to the Knight family, this enabled Jane Austen, her mother, her sister Cassandra and friend Martha Lloyd to take up residence in a house that was part of Edward's Chawton estate. It is now the Jane Austen's House Museum. Austen's years in Chawton were the most productive and successful of her literary career. Her first novel *Sense and Sensibility* was published in 1811, just over two years after she settled in the village, and she went on to revise another previously drafted novel and to write a further three while living there. One of the treasures of the Chawton House Library collection is the manuscript play 'Sir Charles Grandison', an adaptation of Samuel Richardson's novel of the same name, written in Jane Austen's hand. It was probably designed to be acted in private, in front of an audience who knew the source text well, and thus provides useful evidence of the late-eighteenth and early-nineteenth-century vogue for private theatricals. Austen family tradition suggests that the adaptation was dictated to Austen by her niece, Jane Anna Elizabeth ('Anna', 1793–1872), the daughter of her eldest brother James (1765–1843) and a member of the most literary branch of Austen's immediate family.

On 18 November 1814 Jane wrote a lengthy letter to her niece Fanny Knight, of whom she was very fond and to whom she dispensed advice that seems to have been welcome, Fanny's mother having died. The most eye-catching aspect of the letter is the interesting question of whether or not Fanny is in love and, if so, how much. Two unobtrusive lines in it, however, suggest the role of Chawton House in the rhythms of Jane's life at this time. Eager to read the latest news from Fanny in privacy and 'full of curiosity & concern', she remarks: 'Luckily Your

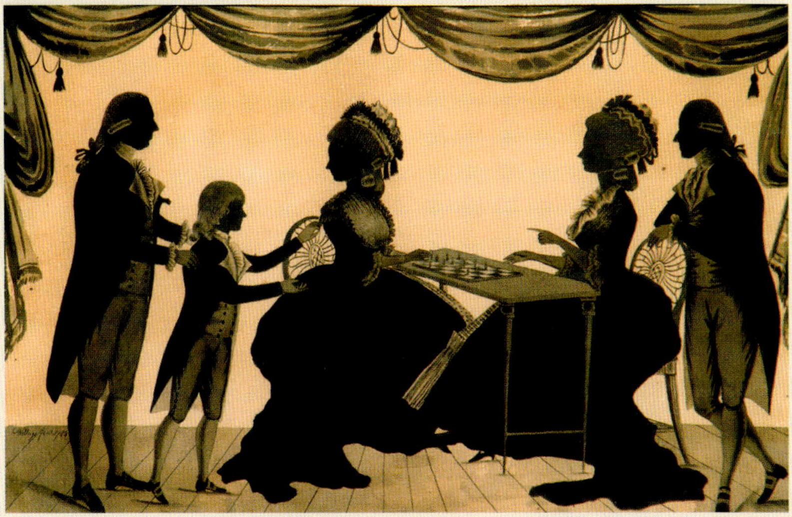

RIGHT *The Reverend George Austen presenting Edward Austen to Mr and Mrs Thomas Knight* by William Wellings, 1783.

BELOW Portrait of Fanny Knight, Jane Austen's niece, by Jeremiah Steele, dated June 1819.

Aunt C. dined at the other house, therefore I had not to manoeuvre away from *her*.' At this time Edward Austen had lent what Jane tended to call 'the Great House' to his brother Francis (Frank) but was paying a visit there himself: 'Aunt Cass: & I dine at the

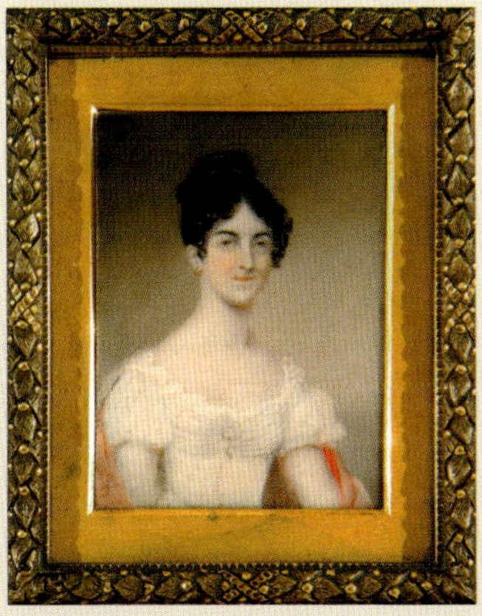

Gt House to day' wrote Jane to Fanny; 'We shall be a snug half dozen'. Evidently home life at Chawton Cottage was sufficiently lacking in privacy that 'getting away by myself' called for ingenuity; visits of one form or another to the Great House provided breathing space and variety. They also clearly afforded the chance to enjoy easy company, a pleasure neatly caught by the word 'snug'.

A portrait of Fanny Knight, later Lady Knatchbull, hangs in the Oak Room. Jane Austen's affection for this young niece was so warm ('You are the delight of my life') that many readers are surprised by Fanny's harsh letter written in later life, many decades after Jane's death, in which she looked back to an aunt who was 'not so refined as she ought to have been from her talent'.

The Long Gallery

'Miss Eliza Bennet, let me persuade you to follow my example, and take a turn about the room. – I assure you it is very refreshing after sitting so long in one attitude.'

Miss Bingley in Jane Austen's *Pride & Prejudice*, 1813

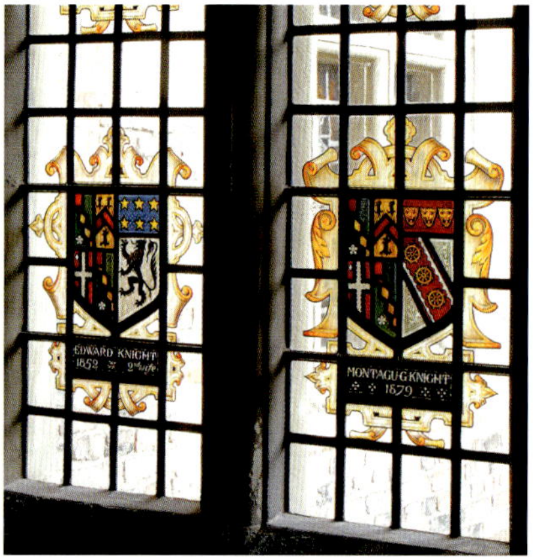

ABOVE Heraldic glass.

OPPOSITE The Long Gallery.

This broad corridor was originally used for exercise by the ladies of the house when the weather kept them indoors. A gallery like this was also traditionally used as a space for the display of family and other portraits, to impress visitors. It is now the main thoroughfare on the first floor, connecting the Upper Reading Room and nearby rooms (all previously bedrooms).

The heraldic stained-glass windows, made by Powell, were added by Montagu Knight between 1910 and 1913. They show the coats of arms of successive freeholders together with their dates of accession. The arms of the St John family start the series, although the first owner at the time of William the Conqueror was Hugh de Port, whose great-grandson married a St John heiress.

A portrait of Elizabeth Knight hangs in the Gallery. Her place in the history of Chawton House turns upon one of many complications in the Knight pedigree, which has not always been lineal and includes many collateral and female descents. When Sir Richard Knight, great-nephew of John Knight, died in 1679, the manor passed in succession to three members of the Martin family, second cousins once removed: Richard, Christopher and finally Elizabeth Martin. Each of them changed their surname to Knight upon inheriting, as did Elizabeth's first and second husbands William Woodward and Bulstrode Peachey. Elizabeth died childless in 1737, having held the manor for thirty-five years. In the absence of a direct heir the manor then passed to another cousin, Thomas Brodnax May (later Knight), whose portrait hangs in the Tapestry Gallery.

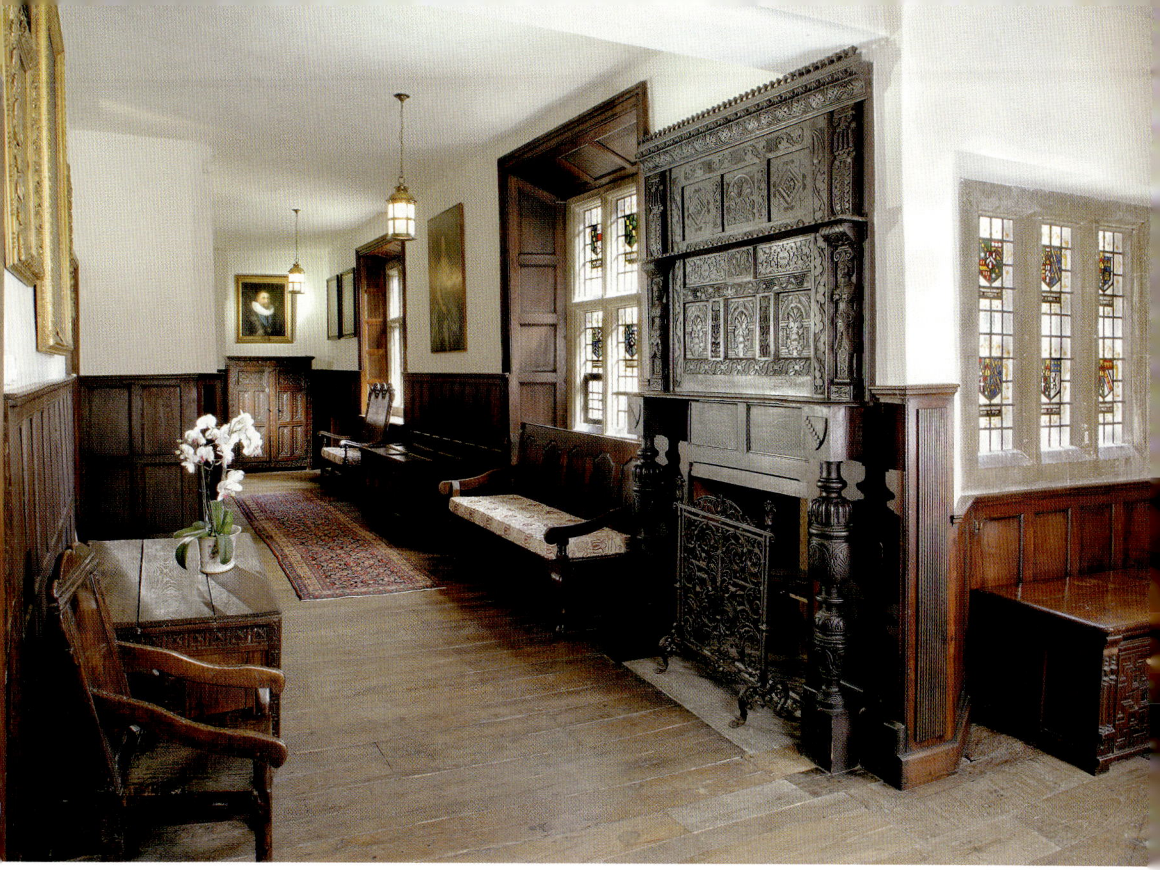

RIGHT Portrait of Elizabeth Knight after Jeremiah Davison, 1733.

FAR RIGHT Portrait of Thomas Knight II attributed to Francis Cotes.

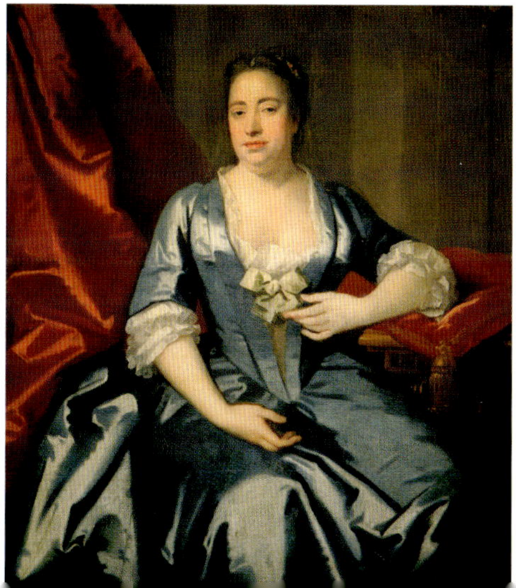

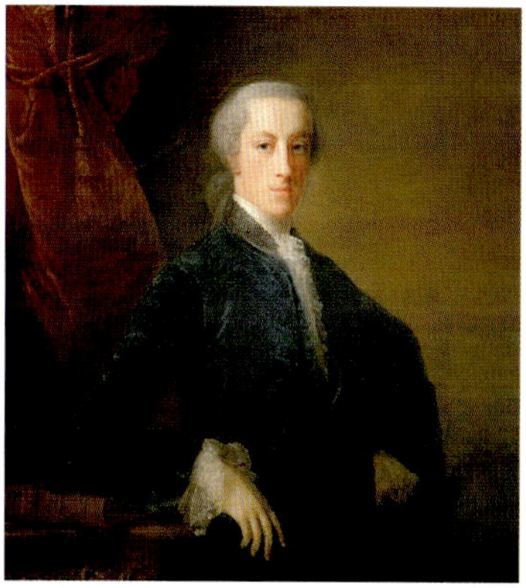

The Great Staircase and Hall

'The artist is an explorer whom nothing ought to stop, and who does neither good nor ill when turning to the right or to the left. His end justifies all.'

George Sand (1804–1876), letter to Gustave Flaubert, 1866

A major remodelling of the house was carried out in about 1655 by Sir Richard Knight, great-nephew of John Knight. The new works introduced Jacobean architectural styles and included the provision of a new hanging staircase to the first and second floors. The staircase is an excellent example of Jacobean woodwork, matched on a magnificent door surround that bears the inscription 'RK 1655'.

The windows include some fine armorial stained glass. These depict the coats of arms of Elizabeth I, Edward Manners the third Earl of Rutland, King Henry II of France, Anthony Browne the first Viscount Montagu, Philip II of Spain, Queen Mary I of England and Edward Knight II.

The portrait on the stairs is of Frances, Countess of Scarborough. The portraits in the Hall are of women writers who engaged with political and philosophical debates. Among these is George Sand, probably France's most famous nineteenth-century female author. Born Aurore Dupin, she became a prolific writer of novels, essays, articles and plays, an accomplished painter and an educator. She was also famously unorthodox in her dress, her love affairs and her extraordinarily wide-ranging friendships. Gustave Flaubert confessed that at Sand's funeral in 1879 'I cried like an ass'.

Painting conservator Caroline Baker had no hesitation in choosing the portrait of Amelia Opie (1769–1853) that hangs in the Staircase Hall as her favourite painting at Chawton House Library, after working to restore lost and flaking paint on the picture. Caroline noted the use of bold colours here, aptly conveying a sense of strong character. The painting is by Opie's husband, the self-taught artist John Opie.

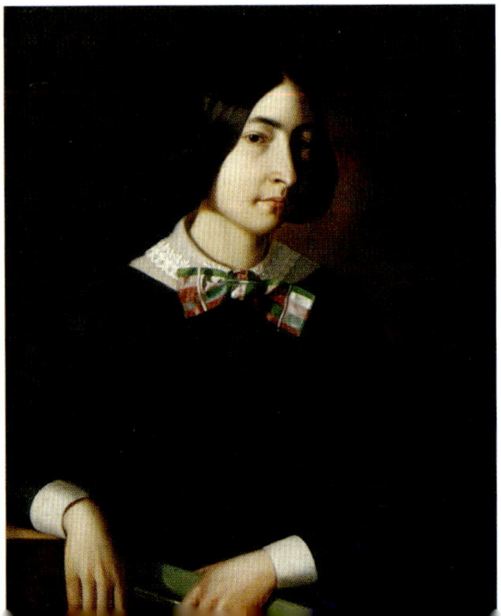

RIGHT Portrait of George Sand by Jean-Baptiste Bizard, 1847.

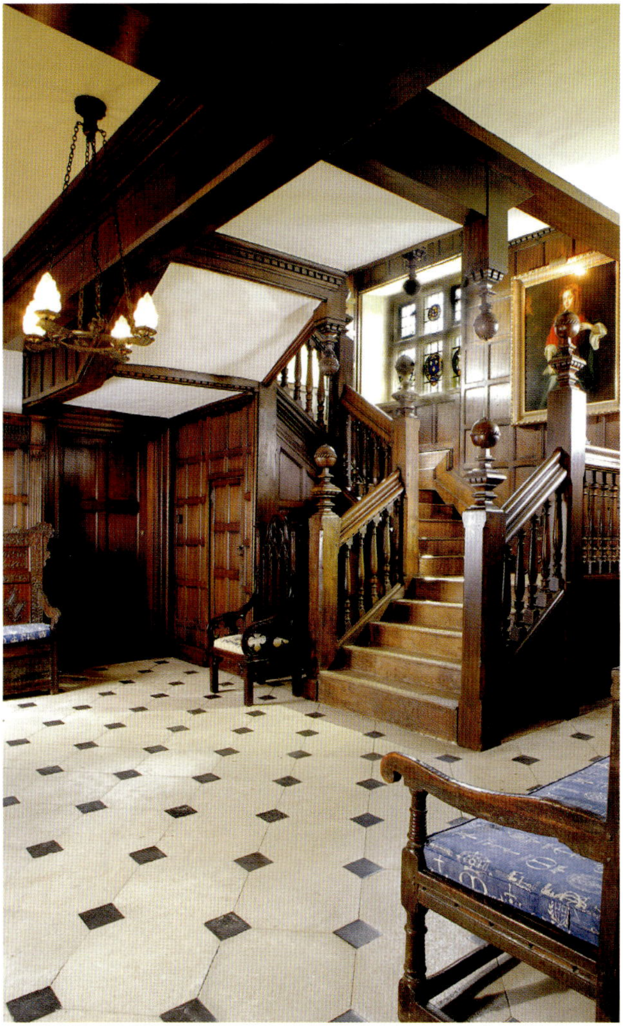

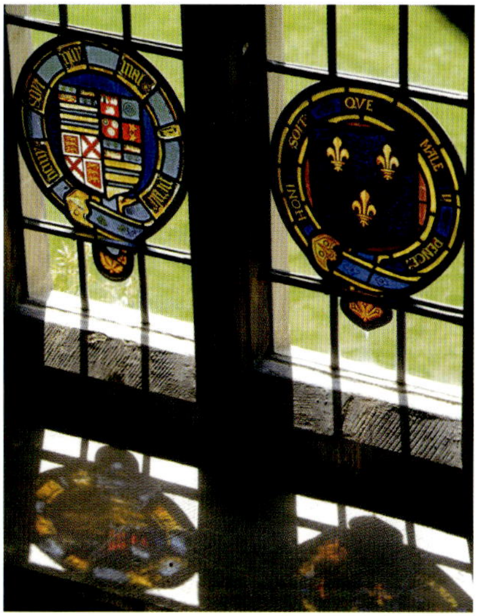

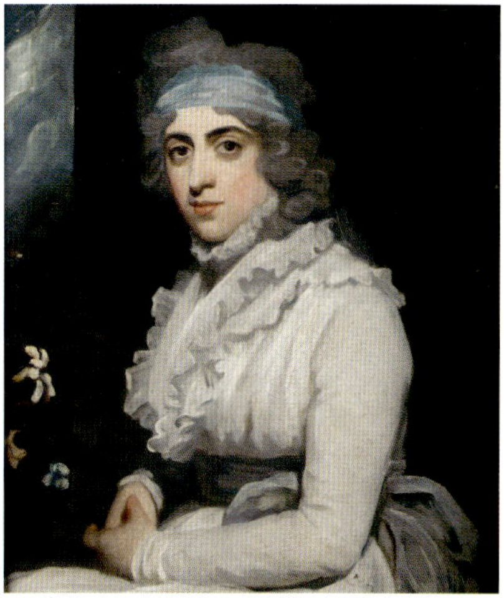

ABOVE The Staircase Hall.

ABOVE RIGHT Armorial stained glass.

RIGHT Portrait of Amelia Opie attributed to her husband, John Opie.

Women as Philosophers and Activists

'Tho various tints the human face adorn
To glorious Liberty Mankind are born;
O, May the hands which rais'd this fav'rite weed
Be loos'd in mercy and the slave be freed'
Mary Knowles (1733–1807), inscription inside a tobacco box, 1788

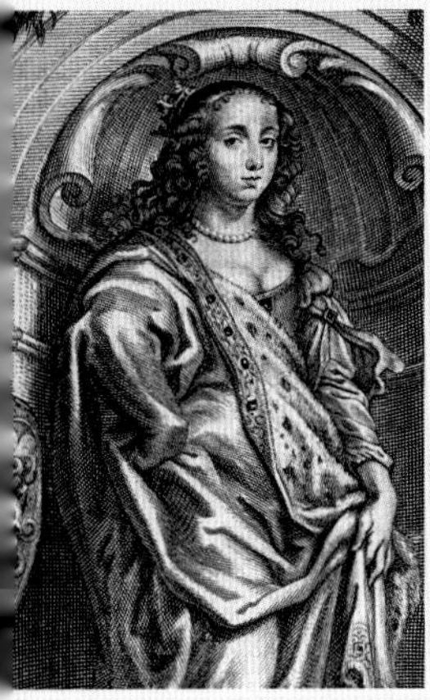

ABOVE This engraved portrait of Margaret Cavendish is a frontispiece to her *Playes*, 1668.

In the Library's collection is an early example of what would now be called an autobiography, *The Adventures of Rivella* (1714) by Delarivier Manley, in which Manley declares that 'Politicks is not the Business of a Woman'. In fact, she was not inclined to leave political writing to men. Throughout the eighteenth century women authors followed suit, writing about key political, moral and social issues. In this, they had an early model in the form of Margaret Cavendish, Duchess of Newcastle (1623–1673), one of the first women writers to publish under her own name, whose work ranged widely across genres and topics. She engaged with other philosophers by critiquing the work of Descartes and Hobbes among others and by exploring contemporary gender relations.

From the other end of the long eighteenth century, a key instance of engagement with fundamental political and philosophical issues is Mary Wollstonecraft's *A Vindication of the Rights of Woman* (1792), a first edition of which is held by the Library. This famous text set out a model for what would today be called 'liberal' feminism based upon the notion of universal human rights explored by Voltaire, Rousseau and Locke, among other Enlightenment figures.

Wollstonecraft was part of a politically radical circle that formed around writer William Godwin and included Amelia Opie. Born to a Dissenting family in Norwich, Opie wrote fiction that deliberately avoided the complex plotting and emphasis upon manners of most novels of the time, instead writing simply structured fiction that considered moral issues and social difference, as did her published poetry. Her novel *Adeline Mowbray, or, the Mother and Daughter* (1804), for example, explored the possibility of men and women living together outside marriage. Her poetry and fiction were warmly received, Sir Walter Scott writing of her novel *The Father and Daughter* (1801) that he 'had cried over it more than he ever cried over such things'.

The poet Mary Knowles (1733–1807), whose portrait hangs in the Entrance Hall, was known as a brilliant conversationalist who sparred verbally

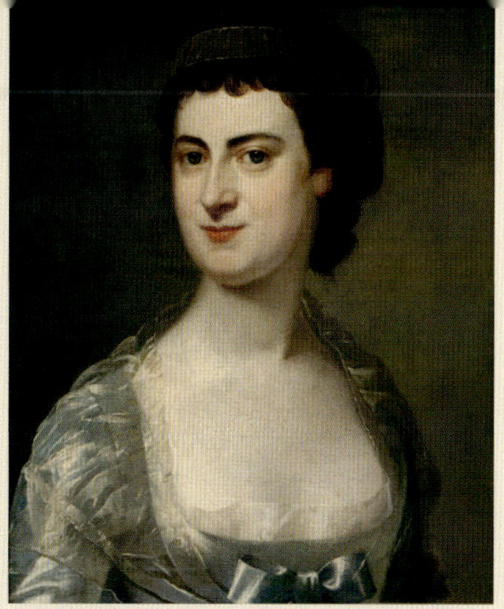

LEFT Portrait of Mary Knowles attributed to William Hoare.

BELOW Hannah More's *The Sorrows of Yamba*, c.1795.

with Samuel Johnson. In 1799 she published an account of her debate with him over Quakerism, which James Boswell had declined to include in his biography of Johnson.

Writers like these engaged from the beginning in the movement for the abolition of slavery. The literary output of the philanthropist, evangelical and member of the bluestocking circle Hannah More (1756–1833) included cheap, affordable literature that carried an obvious moral message. In the Library's collection is a poem published by More in the form of a broadside or single sheet of large size, called *The Sorrows of Yamba; or, the Negro Woman's Lamentation* (*c.*1795). Written in the voice of an enslaved woman, the poem describes both the agony of the enforced separation of mother and child and the comfort of religious faith. Women were active in promoting a boycott of sugar grown on plantations using slave labour, and in large numbers they subscribed to the Abolition Society. However, it did not escape the notice of women intellectuals that they were not permitted to hold office in organisations like this, and their writing increasingly drew parallels between the evil of slavery and their own disenfranchisement. After the Abolition Act, passed in 1807, which abolished the slave trade but not chattel slavery (a child born to an enslaved person was still a slave), women were instrumental in keeping the movement alive.

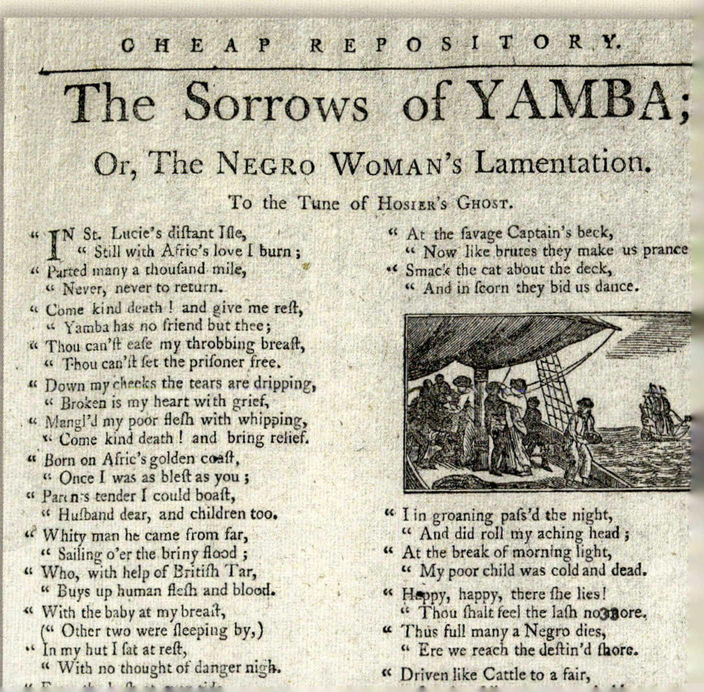

CHEAP REPOSITORY.

The Sorrows of YAMBA;

Or, The NEGRO WOMAN'S Lamentation.

To the Tune of HOSIER'S GHOST.

" IN St. Lucie's diſtant Iſle,
" Still with Afric's love I burn;
" Parted many a thouſand mile,
" Never, never to return.
" Come kind death! and give me reſt,
" Yamba has no friend but thee;
" Thou can'ſt eaſe my throbbing breaſt,
" Thou can'ſt ſet the priſoner free.
" Down my cheeks the tears are dripping,
" Broken is my heart with grief,
" Mangl'd my poor fleſh with whipping,
" Come kind death! and bring relief.
" Born on Afric's golden coaſt,
" Once I was as bleſt as you;
" Parents tender I could boaſt,
" Huſband dear, and children too.
" Whity man he came from far,
" Sailing o'er the briny flood;
" Who, with help of Britiſh Tar,
" Buys up human fleſh and blood.
" With the baby at my breaſt,
(" Other two were ſleeping by,)
" In my hut I ſat at reſt,
" With no thought of danger nigh.

" At the ſavage Captain's beck,
" Now like brutes they make us prance
" Smack the cat about the deck,
" And in ſcorn they bid us dance.

" I in groaning paſs'd the night,
" And did roll my aching head;
" At the break of morning light,
" My poor child was cold and dead.
" Happy, happy, there ſhe lies!
" Thou ſhalt feel the laſh no more.
" Thus full many a Negro dies,
" Ere we reach the deſtin'd ſhore.
" Driven like Cattle to a fair,

Lower Reading Room

'...to enjoy that perfect Tranquillity of Life, which is nowhere to be found but in Retreat, a faithful Friend and a good Library.'

Aphra Behn (1640–1689) *The Lucky Mistake*, 1689

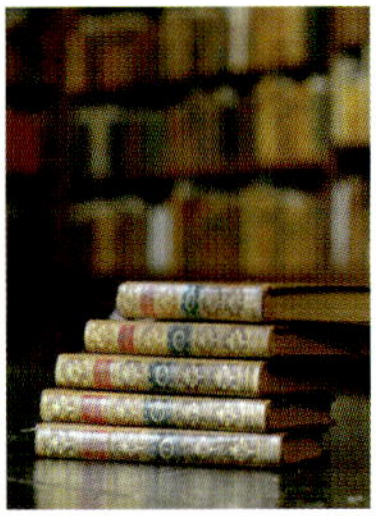

In the late-Victorian period this room was the Knight family Library. Today it accommodates part of Chawton House Library's main collection. The books housed in the Lower Reading Room tend to be those published after 1790; the oldest books in the Library's collection are stored in the Cellar Storeroom.

The tapestry hanging behind the librarian's desk is of a Flemish game park, *c.*1600. The gap in the panelling was for the larger armorial carpet celebrating the Lewknor family (see p.18).

There are many treasures in this room, but the Library's copy of *Julia de Gramont, by the Right Honorable Lady H***** (1788) is particularly interesting. This novel was written by Cassandra Hawke, a cousin of Jane Austen. In her diary, Frances Burney recalled being introduced to Hawke as a 'sister authoress' and having to listen as Hawke quoted some particularly sentimental content from *Julia de Gramont*; Burney took the earliest possible opportunity to 'make away from this terrible set'. The Library's copy of the novel

ABOVE The Lower Reading Room.

RIGHT Jane Eaton's panoramic sketch in Charlotte Eaton's *The Battle of Waterloo*, 1815, depicting the site of the battle.

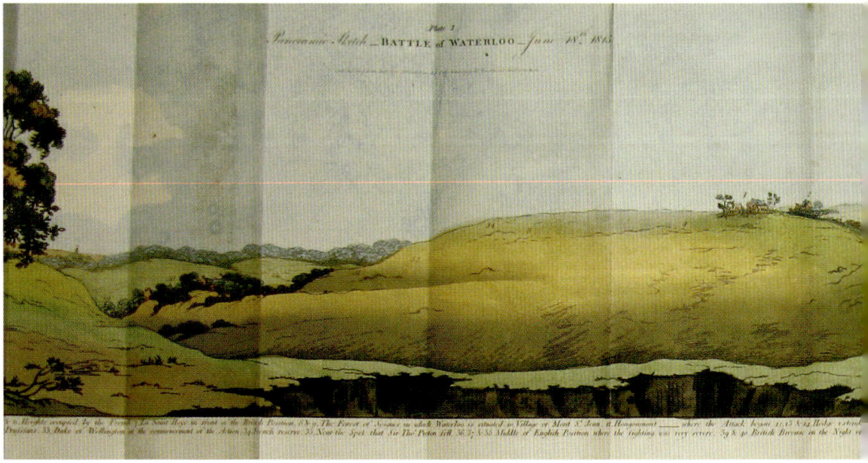

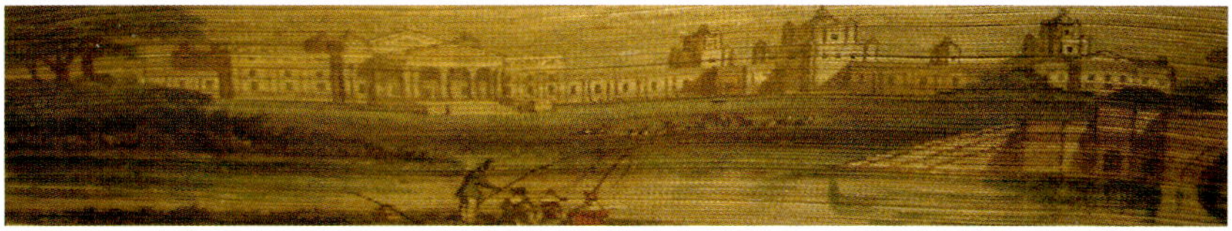

ABOVE Fore-edge painting, Cassandra Hawke's *Julia de Gramont*, 1788.

bears an armorial bookplate belonging to Hawke's son, and its two volumes have an exquisite secret. Concealed beneath the gilded edges of its pages are delicate paintings of Blenheim Palace in Oxfordshire and Grimsthorpe Castle in Lincolnshire. These images, called hidden fore-edge paintings, reveal themselves only when the leaves of the volume are fanned in a particular way.

Another remarkable book in this room is a first-hand account of the Battle of Waterloo by 'a near Observer', Charlotte Eaton, who, along with her sister Jane, found herself caught up in the horrors of war during a trip to Belgium with their brother. Their stay in Brussels, where the Duke of Wellington and his army were temporarily stationed, was interrupted when the French army advanced on the city. Having woken to the sound of bugles, within hours the little group had decided to flee amidst the sound of nearby canon fire, taking two injured soldiers with them in their carriage. A month later, they returned to Brussels and visited the field of Waterloo where they were appalled by the countless fresh graves and scattered debris. Here Jane sketched a stunning panorama of the landscape, cleansed of all the shocking signs of violence. It is reproduced in the book as a wide fold-out.

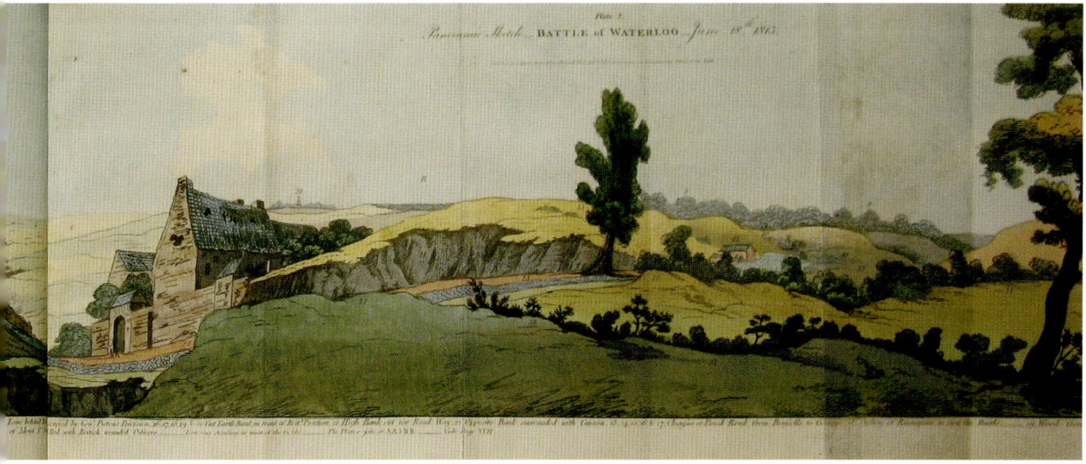

The Servants' Passage

'The performance of your duty ought to constitute your chief pleasure; and it will only render you unhappy, and make you an unprofitable servant if you set your mind upon holyday-making, and look upon your duty as drudgery and confinement.'

The Duties of a Lady's Maid (anonymous), 1825

The Servants' Passage was added in 1655 in order to allow household staff to pass between the north and south wings without crossing the Great Hall. It also provides access to the original brick wine cellars and to several basements. A log store, accessible from both the Passage and the Great Hall, was introduced to allow servants to replenish the supply of logs to the Great Hall without disturbing its occupants. The archway leading into the Passage from the main part of the house dates from the eighteenth century, whilst in the nineteenth century a document safe was fitted in the Passage in place of the former garderobe (latrine) from the main Bedroom Chamber above the Great Hall.

The 1861 census return for Chawton House, then headed by Edward Knight II and his wife Adela, records the presence of a number of female relatives, a governess for the children and a large number of servants. Some were local but others were surprisingly far from their place of birth: for instance, among the laundry-maids were Mary Goodchild, aged sixteen, from Chawton and Elizabeth Doughty from Holy Island, County Durham (in North East England). A majority of the servants were under the age of thirty, but Elizabeth Doughty was still performing her heavy duties in the laundry aged fifty-eight.

From today's perspective, very little about a servant's life seems amusing, but items in the Library's collection remind us that, historically, idle and rascally servants were stock comic figures. George Cruikshank provided twelve vigorous illustrations for Henry and Augustus Mayhew's *The Greatest Plague of Life: or the Adventures of a Lady in Search of a Good Servant* (1847), a comic novel satirising the inexperienced housewife's search for reliable domestic help that remained in print until 1892.

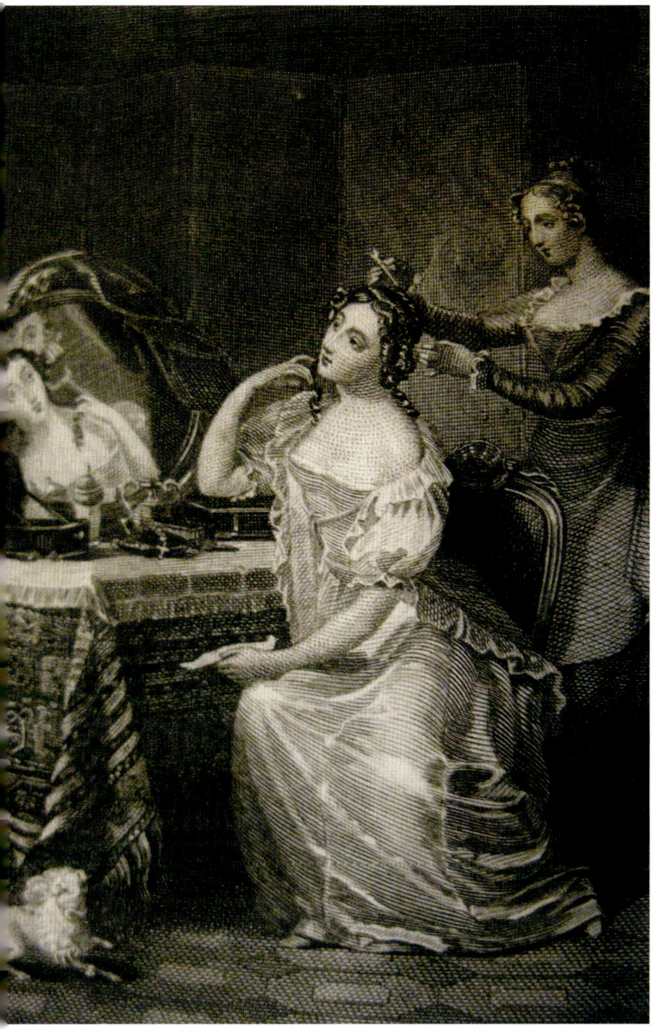

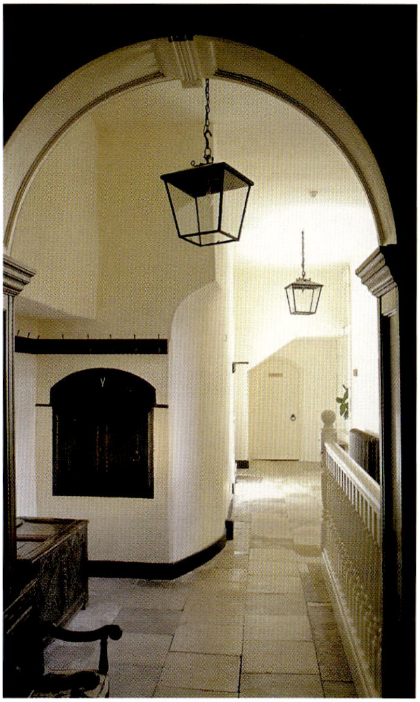

ABOVE The Servants' Passage.

LEFT *Belinda at her Toilet*: frontispiece engraving in *The Duties of a Lady's Maid*, 1825, republished by Chawton House Library in 2015.

The Old Kitchen

'But now her Dish-kettle began
To boil and blubber with the foaming Bran.
The greasy Apron round her Hips she ties,
And to each Plate the scalding Clout applies:
The purging Bath each glowing Dish refines,
And once again the polish'd Pewter shines.'

Mary Leapor (1722–1746), *Crumble Hall*, 1751

BELOW The Old Kitchen.

The Old Kitchen, built in 1592, is at the heart of a cluster of spaces where the servants carried out their work, including the Scullery, Wine Cellar, Game Larder, Well House and Pump Room. The early Victorian range set into a brick alcove is marked 'Flavel & Company, Patent, prize Kitchener, Leamington'. The other kitchen fittings include a late-Georgian dresser, a copper for boiling water and two coffee grinders attached to a timber post above the work-table. The table itself dates from the eighteenth century and has been worn to an uneven surface by centuries of chopping and scrubbing.

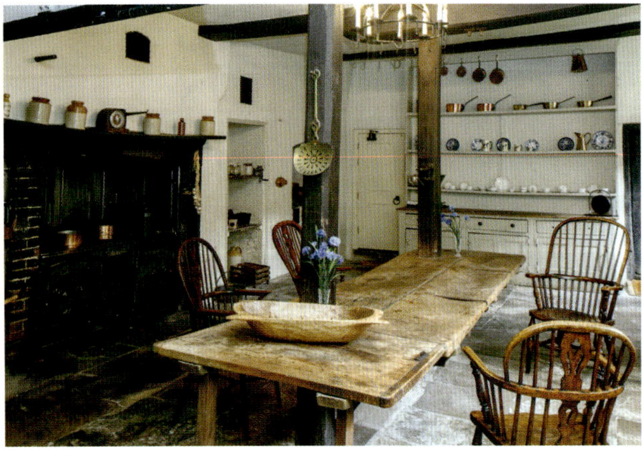

A Knight family recipe book inscribed 'This book I brought from Chawton and gave to my sister Mrs. J. Knight, on whose death it was returned – TK 1793' is a particularly precious survival that gives us an insight into the products of the kitchen in the eighteenth century. Two separate hands appear to have compiled it, their identities now unknown. Alongside recipes for orange wine and 'ragoo' are instructions on the making of household remedies, 'a water to make the hair grow thick' for example. The Library's collection includes a number of works that similarly juxtapose the culinary and the medicinal. One volume in which two texts have been bound together – *A Choice Manuall, or rare and select secrets in Physick and Chyrurgery* (1653) by Elizabeth, Countess of Kent and *A True Gentlewoman's Delight* (also 1653) – is on a miniature scale suited to being carried in a pocket. In contrast, an anonymous late-seventeenth-century

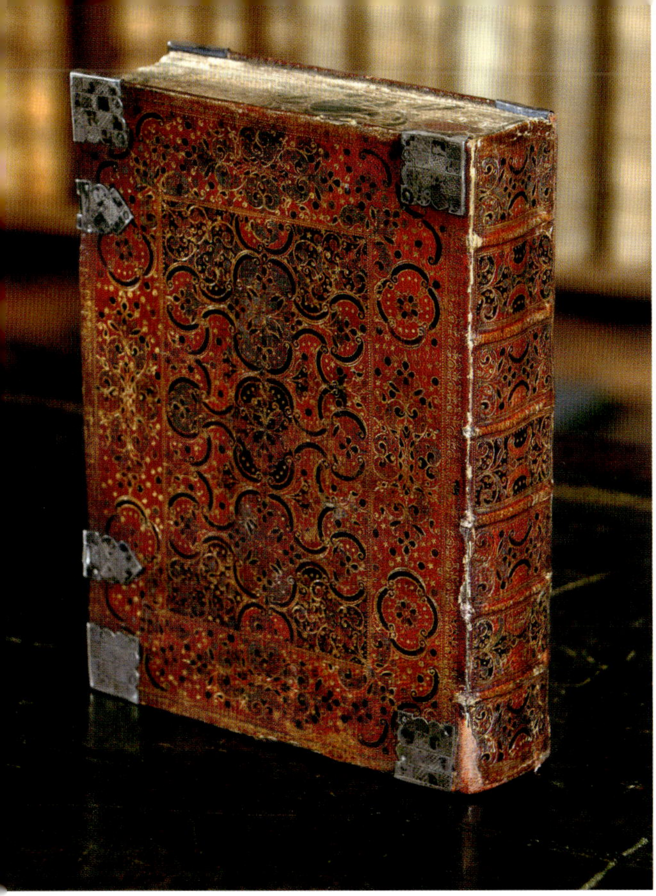

ABOVE The fine binding of an anonymous late-seventeenth-century recipe book.

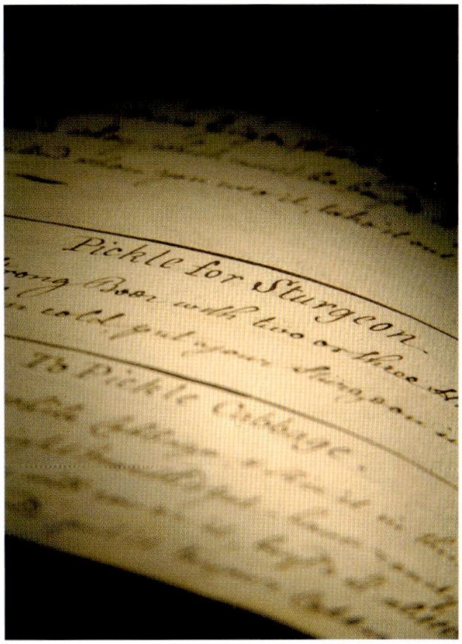

RIGHT The Knight family cookbook.

manuscript recipe book seems unlikely to have been used on the move; its spectacular red morocco binding suggests that this volume was consulted well away from the domestic offices.

The Kitchen leads to a Scullery equipped with large stone and slate sinks for rough kitchen work and a large chopping block. The sinks were supplied with water pumped from the nearby Well House, which dates from the 1580s or earlier. A steam-driven pump was installed by Alfred Hetherington of Alton in around 1850.

The Well House is located next to the Game Larder, whose hooked beams were marked with the days of the week, sometimes spelled idiosyncratically, to help monitor hanging times. The room above the Game Larder is a later addition and was used for many years as a children's Nursery, connected by a flying corridor (since demolished) to the staff accommodation above the Kitchen.

Women in Service and in Print

'We must make haste, for when we Home are come,
Alas! We find our Work but just begun;
So many Things for our Attendance call,
Had we ten Hands, we could employ them all…
You Sup, and go to Bed without delay,
And rest yourselves till the ensuing Day;
While we alas! But little Sleep can have
Because our forward Children cry and rave;
Yet, without fail, soon as Day-light doth spring,
We in the field again our Work begin.'

Mary Collier (*c.*1690–*c.*1762), *The Woman's Labour*, 1739

RIGHT Title page from Mary Leapor's *Poems upon Several Occasions*, 1748.

OPPOSITE LEFT TO RIGHT Staircase leading to the attic rooms, which were probably servants' quarters.

Hooked beams in the game larder were marked with days of the week to monitor hanging times.

The centuries-old kitchen table is worn from years of behind-the-scenes labour.

Astonishingly, in the eighteenth century a handful of labouring men and women succeeded in publishing their writing, often with assistance from a patron. Relatively well-known examples are Stephen Duck, dubbed 'the labouring poet', and Ann Yearsley, 'the Bristol milkwoman', whose literary cause was taken up by Hannah More. The careers of both poets were tinged with sadness; Yearsley broke with More over the handling of the proceeds of her publications, and Duck took his own life.

Poet Mary Collier, who lived not far from Chawton in Petersfield and later in Alton, was employed for most of her life in 'Washing, Brewing and such labour, still devoting what leisure time I had to books'. Printed in a pamphlet costing sixpence, her poem *The Woman's Labour* (1739) apparently earned very little for Collier herself, as 'others run away with the profit'. The poem was a response to Stephen Duck's poem *The Thresher's Labour* (1730), which appeared to belittle working-class women's labour in comparison's to men's, and to denigrate 'prattling females'. Collier's emphasis on equality, and on the dual nature of women's labour in the field and in the home, has led scholars to point out her importance as an early feminist.

Mary Leapor toiled first in the gardens of a Northamptonshire estate and later as a cook-maid for a gentry family. She gained the support of a local rector's daughter who began to organise

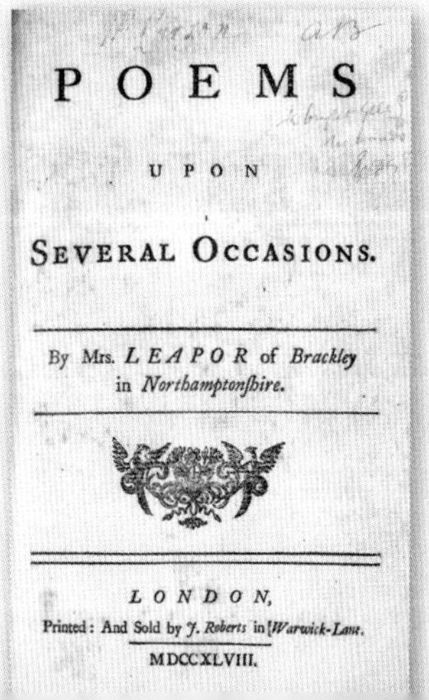
POEMS

UPON

SEVERAL OCCASIONS.

By Mrs. *LEAPOR* of *Brackley* in *Northamptonshire.*

LONDON,

Printed: And Sold by *J. Roberts* in *Warwick-Lane.*

MDCCXLVIII.

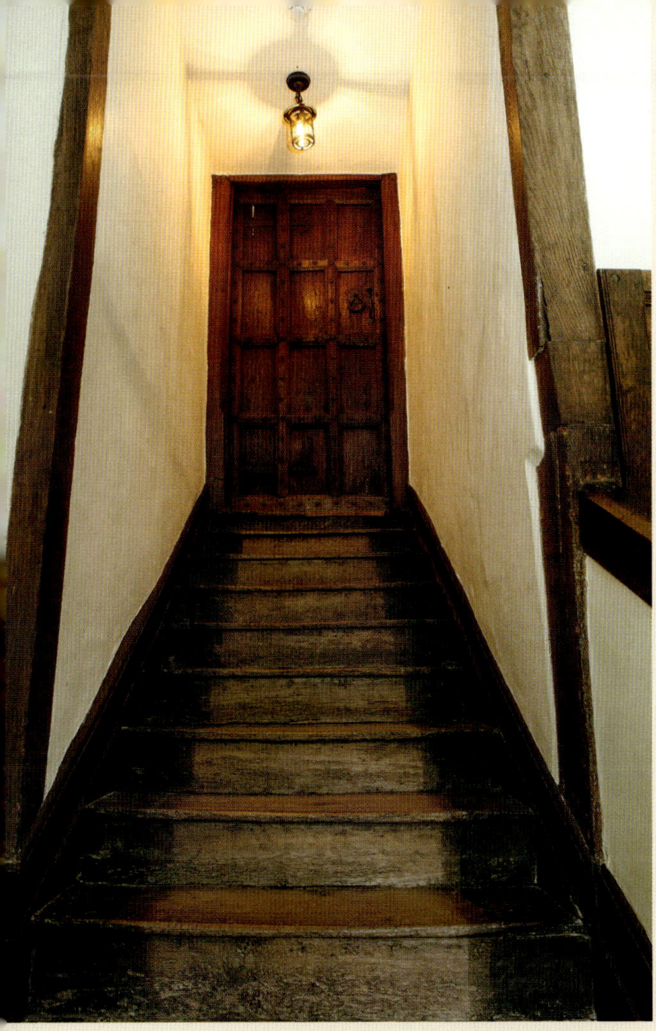

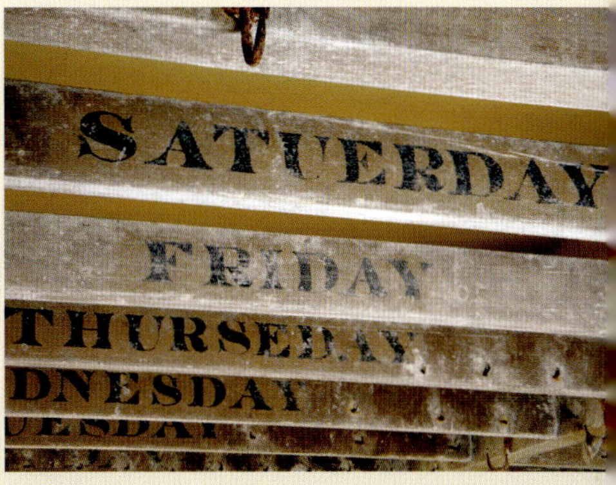

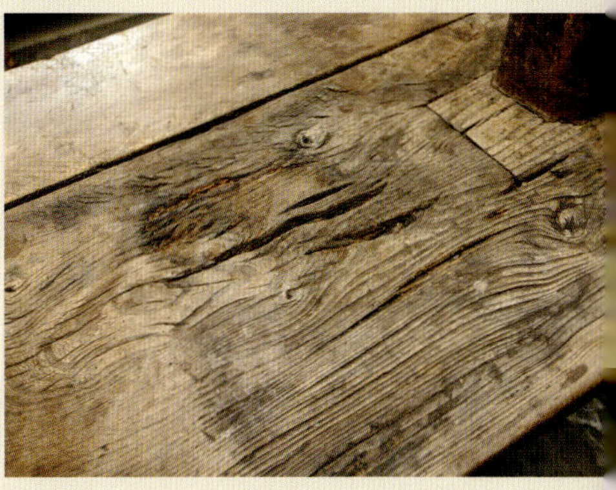

a subscription for the publication of her poems. After Leapor's death from measles at the age of twenty-four, the plan to print her *Poems upon Several Occasions* came to fruition; this volume (1748) is in the collection at Chawton House Library. Three years later Samuel Richardson's determination to see more of Leapor's poems in print resulted in a second volume. The best-known of her poems, *Crumble Hall*, subverts the convention of the country-house poem by describing in stark detail the below-stairs toil upon which the whole edifice relied.

Behind the Scenes

'Often when I think myself miles away from one part of the house I find a passage or entrance close to it, & I don't know when I shall be quite mistress of all the intricate, & different ways.'

Fanny Knight (1793–1882), letter to Miss Chapman, 1807

BELOW The Upper Reading Room. The portrait above the fireplace is thought to be of Sarah Harriet Burney by a follower of Thomas Lawrence.

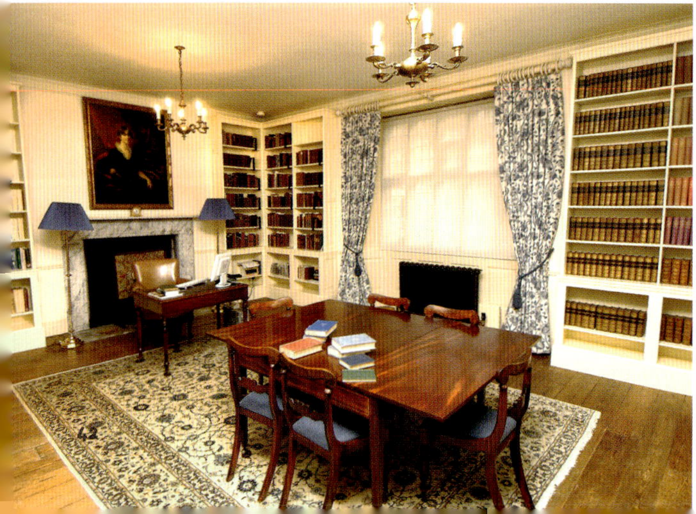

The Upper Reading Room, at one time a bedroom, is one of Chawton House Library's two main reading rooms. An additional collection of critical and biographical material that supports the early and rare texts is kept here. The Library's Visiting Fellows, who come from all over the world to study at the Library, are given desk space to work in the Upper Reading Room, usually for up to a month.

It has been suggested that the portrait hanging in the Upper Reading Room is of Sarah Harriet Burney (1772–1844). Burney, younger half-sister of the better-known Frances, was a successful novelist in her own right. She published five works in her lifetime: *Traits of Nature* (1812), whose heroine is, like its author, the child of a difficult second marriage, sold particularly well, with three editions by 1813. The Library has copies of all five titles including first editions of *Clarentine* (1796), *Geraldine Falconberg* (1808) and *The Romance of Private Life* (1839). The Austen family read this author's work; we know that they read *Clarentine* three times. For her part, Sarah Harriet read *Emma* with 'glee' and called *Pride and Prejudice* (1813) 'my prime favourite of all modern Novels'.

The Maids' Sitting Room, now used primarily for meetings and storage, is so named due to its use in later years. It features wall-to-wall wood panelling, and one wall is taken up with cupboards and drawers, which are likely to be late Georgian or early Victorian; these feature pull-out shelves for storing linen. During restoration work, a George III florin was found under the floorboards, the loss of which may have been much lamented by its owner!

The Cellar Storeroom is where, prior to the restoration of the house, the

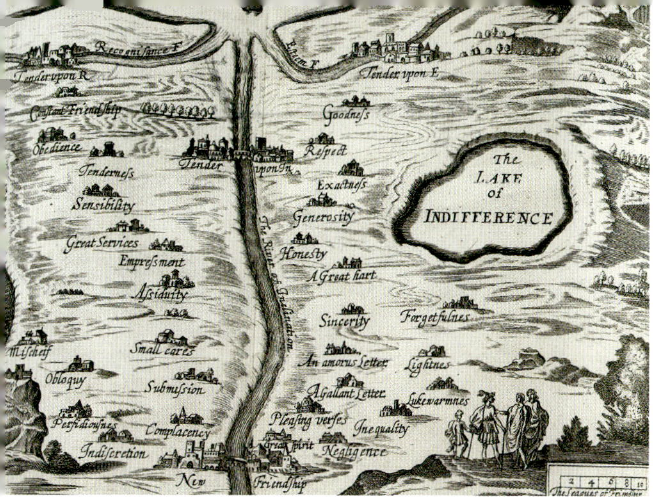

ABOVE The 'Carte de Tendre' – the map of romance – in *Clelia, an Excellent New Romance* by Madeleine de Scudéry, 1678.

BELOW The Maid's Sitting Room.

records of the Knight family were found in a waterlogged and largely unreadable state. In most cases, the damage was irreparable, but the papers did tell of a period of considerable activity between 1707 and 1709 when trees were cleared and brick walls built in the garden, which necessitated 'digging and cleansing 65,000 bricks'. Today, the more fragile books and those published before *c.*1790 are generally kept in the Cellar Storeroom.

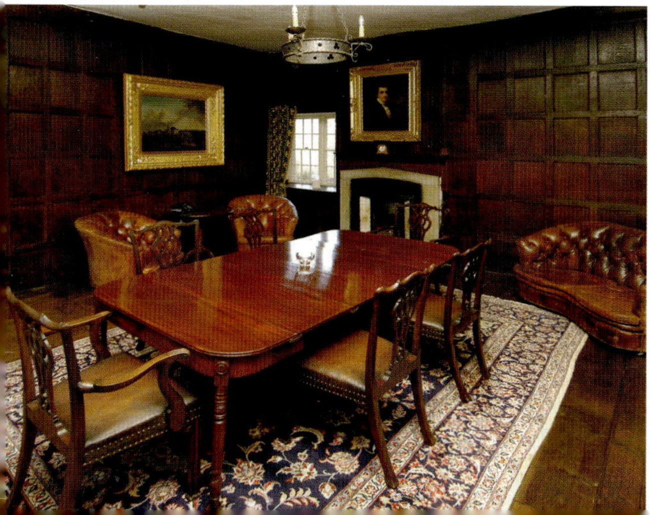

Both the Lower Reading Room and the Storeroom are kept at a temperature of 18–20°C and a humidity of 45–55%, which is optimal for books of this age.

One of the jewels of the collection kept here is *Clelia, an Excellent New Romance* (1678) by Madeleine de Scudéry (1608–1701), a translation from the French original *Clélie, histoire romaine.* Scudéry's Romances met with an enthusiastic response from readers across the Channel in Britain, although they have been largely forgotten by twenty-first-century readers. The seventeenth-century Romance was the forerunner of the novel as we now know it. The genre typically includes lengthy conversations and diversions, with fantastical beasts, mythical creatures, and trials and tribulations of all kinds for the heroine. *Clelia* includes a fascinating map of the landscape of the Romance, the 'Carte de Tendre', depicting a mythical land where the topography is named using the language of love.

The Attic of the house now contains offices. Very little is known about how this space was used, although it is likely that in later years it served as the servants' quarters. The rooms, with their sloping ceilings, small fireplaces and individual features, have great character.

The Gardens and Estate

'Edward is very well and enjoys himself as well as any Hampshire born Austen can desire. – He talks of making a new Garden; the present is a bad one & ill situated, near Mr Papillon's; – he means to have the new, at the top of the Lawn behind his own house.'

Jane Austen, letter to her brother Francis, 1813

Mellichamp's painting of Chawton House (*c.*1740; see p. 19) shows formal gardens based on geometric shapes, possibly derived from the original Elizabethan gardens. At this date, as well as the terraced gardens with topiary, there were two avenues, a kitchen garden and a 'wilderness'. Between 1763 and 1785 the formal element of the garden was swept away to be replaced by parkland in the English Landscape style popular at the time. Practitioners of this approach to landscaping advocated surrounding a house with seemingly natural lawns grazed by animals discreetly held back from the house by a 'ha-ha' or ditch that was invisible from a distance. At Chawton House Library, the landscape of this period has been restored, with an informal lawn and open views to the south west (complete with ha-ha). This setting is a key element of the house's charm and provides a fitting context for the library's aims.

The house has a gravel path on its south side, lawns leading to the wilderness, and a lime avenue that provides distant views into the parkland beyond. The idea of a wilderness went back to the seventeenth century, when the appeal of a wooded area that appeared natural but was in fact artificially planted and tended took hold. The desirability of a wilderness survived the transition to the English Landscape style, and it remained a feature of eighteenth-century garden design.

The gravel path connects to a small garden – the Library Terrace – and on to a serpentine path that leads to the Upper Terrace. The Library Terrace was built in about 1905 on the site of an early-nineteenth-century conservatory. Both terraces were built by Montagu Knight and bear evidence of the influence of Sir Edwin Lutyens who was a close friend. At the highest point of the grounds is the Walled Garden, built by Edward Austen (later Knight) between 1818 and 1822 and accessed via fine wrought-iron gates. Although converted in the early 1900s to a flower garden, originally it was created as a kitchen garden with fruit trees growing against the walls and apple trees and soft fruits planted alternately within a rectangular design. This is the garden to which Jane Austen refers in the quotation above; she did not live to see its completion.

While Jane Austen can be assumed to have spent much time in the gardens, the extent to which they influenced the settings of her novels remains uncertain. The backdrop of the South Downs and Hampshire is certainly characteristic of many of her novels, particularly *Emma*, in which some believe Highbury to be modelled upon Alton and Mr Knightley's Donwell Abbey upon Chawton House.

The Chawton House estate currently extends to about 275 acres (111 hectares). Shire horses help to maintain the estate in an environmentally friendly way. The horses have been trained to carry out traditional agricultural work, and their hooves are less damaging to flora and fauna than modern machinery. In earlier times the estate's horses would have been stabled in the 1593 stable-block, one of the finest of its kind in England and now converted to accommodation for the use of the Library's Visiting Fellows and other distinguished guests. Next to the stables are an eighteenth-century dovecote and barn. The Church of St Nicholas, opposite the stables, was rebuilt in 1871. The church retains many memorials to the Knight and Austen families, and Jane Austen's mother and sister are buried in the churchyard.

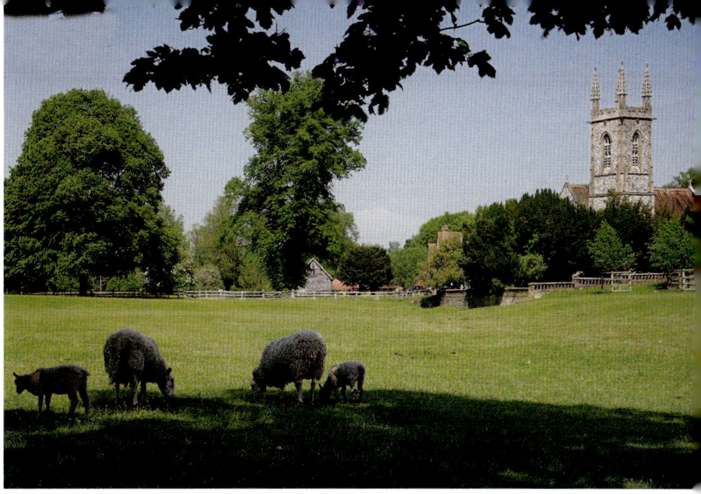

ABOVE The estate encompasses around 275 acres.

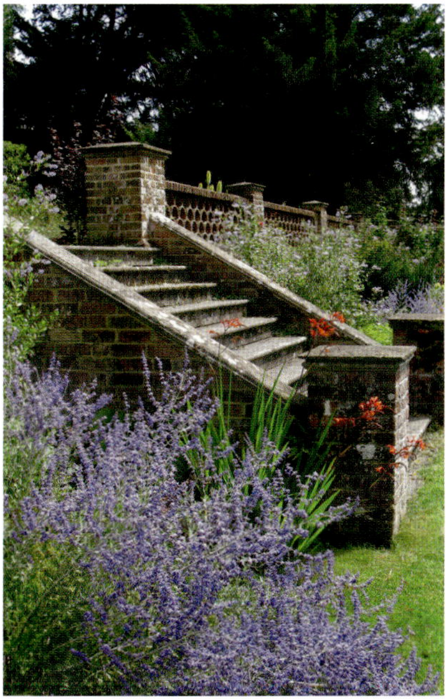

LEFT The Upper Terrace.

Botanical Women

'This work has met with a more favourable reception from the publick, both at home and abroad, than I could have expected, knowing my own insufficiency for the undertaking.'

Elizabeth Blackwell (1700–1758), preface to *A Curious Herbal*, 1737–9

The eighteenth century was a period in which botany came to the fore as a field of scientific enquiry. Both the mother and the wife of George III, Princess Augusta and Queen Charlotte respectively, took a keen interest in botany, the former galvanising the establishment of the Royal Botanic Gardens at Kew in 1759. Mary Wollstonecraft supported the study of botany as a way of improving women's and children's understanding of the natural world, but she decried the association of women with flowers that constructed femininity as decorative rather than useful or practical.

In desperate circumstances, Elizabeth Blackwell conceived and carried out an extraordinary project to write and illustrate *A Curious Herbal... Engraved on Folio Copper Plates... By Elizabeth Blackwell* (1737–9). Identifying the need for a herbal depicting plants from the New World, Blackwell published her work in weekly parts over the course of two years, using the proceeds to secure her husband's release from debtors' prison. The plants were drawn from life

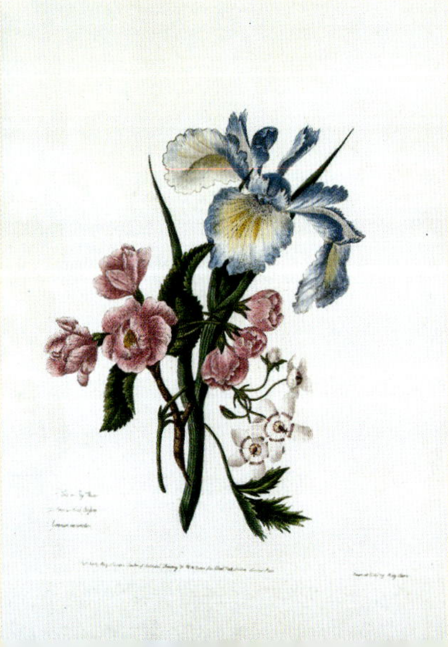

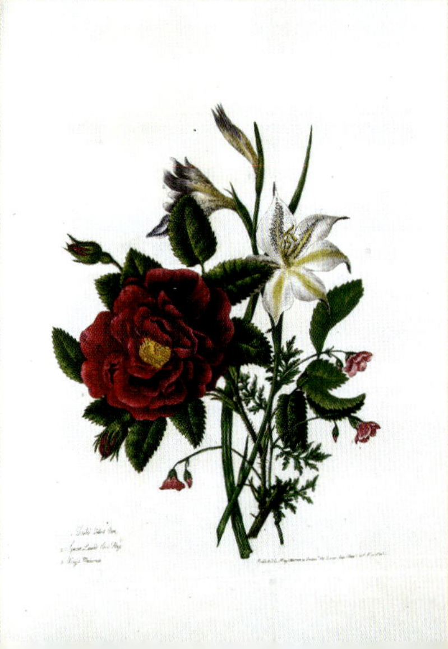

RIGHT Hand-coloured etchings with line and stipple engraving from Mary Lawrance's *Sketches of Flowers from Nature*, 1801

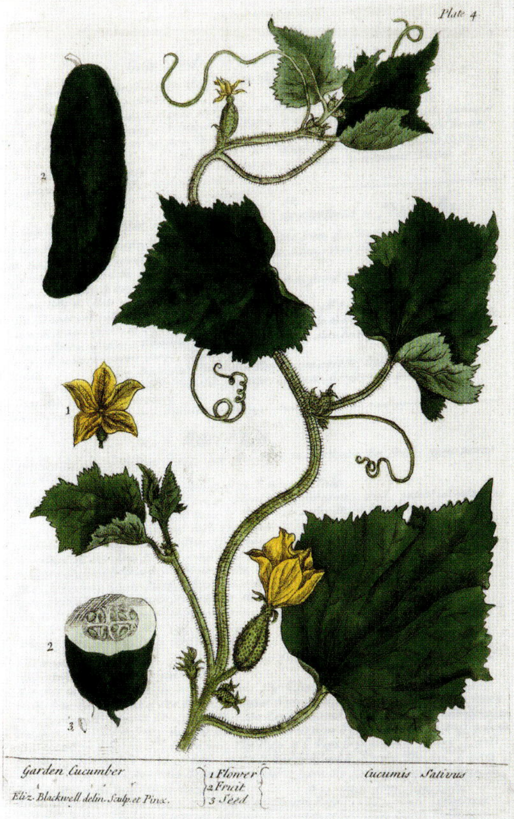

ABOVE Hand-coloured engraving from Elizabeth Blackwell's *A Curious Herbal*, 1737.

at the Chelsea Physic Garden, Blackwell taking a house in nearby Swan Walk in order to be close at hand. She made no other known foray into the graphic arts, and relied on influential patrons to endorse her work. The success of her venture did not prevent her husband from coming to an unfortunate end, for although she earned him his freedom, he was later executed in Sweden for his part in a supposed political intrigue there. The appearance of a number of pirated versions of the Herbal was an ironic compliment to Blackwell's work. The engravings in Chawton House Library's copy have been coloured by hand. In 2016, an Elizabeth Blackwell herb garden was devised and planted in the Walled Garden in homage to Blackwell's work.

London-based Mary Lawrance (fl. 1794–1830) exhibited a flower painting at the Royal Academy in 1795 and went on to publish *A Collection of Roses from Nature* (1796–9) and *Sketches of Flowers from Nature* (1801). *A Collection of Passion Flowers Coloured from Natur*e followed in 1802. She supplemented her earnings from these books by giving lessons in botanical drawing at a charge of half a guinea per lesson plus an entrance fee of one guinea. After marriage (to Thomas Kearse) she continued to exhibit her flower paintings. The horticulturist Robert Sweet, a friend, named a rose after her: *rosa lawranceana*. Chawton House Library's copy of *Sketches of Flowers from Nature* contains eleven etchings with line and stipple engraving, some uncoloured, some with the first layer of wash colouring, and some fully coloured.

First published in 2016 by
Scala Arts & Heritage Publishers Ltd
10 Lion Yard, Tremadoc Road
London SW4 7NQ, UK
www.scalapublishers.com
In association with Chawton House Library
www.chawtonhouselibrary.org

ISBN 978-1-78551-036-6

Text by Helen Cole with help from Staff, Trustees, Friends and Volunteers of Chawton House Library.
Edited by Esme West and Helen Thirlway
Designed by Andrew Barron
Printed in China

10 9 8 7 6 5 4 3 2 1

Front cover: Chawton House Library.
Front inside cover: Books that are only known to exist at Chawton House Library.
Back inside cover: Chawton House Library.
Back cover: *Mary Robinson*, 'Perdita', by John Hoppner, *c.*1782.
Back flap: Hand-coloured engraving from Elizabeth Blackwell's *A Curious Herbal*, 1737.